Memorias De Mi Familia
Memories of My Family

By Michael R. Garcia

Publisher's Cataloging-in-Publication data

Names: Garcia, Michael R., author.
Title: Memorias de mi familia ; Memories of my family / Michael R. Garcia.
Description: Includes bibliographical references. | Pueblo West, CO: Carcel Publishing, 2022.
Identifiers: ISBN 978-1-957077-02-4
Subjects: LCSH Garcia family. | Vigil family. | Southwest, New--History. | West (U.S.)--History. | BISAC REFERENCE / Genealogy & Heraldry | HISTORY / United States / State & Local / West (AK, CA, CO, HI, ID, MT, NV, UT, WY)
Classification: LCC F786 .G37 2022 | DDC 979/092--dc23

Front cover: Bottom – Jose Amarante Garcia & Teodora Espinosa Garcia. Top – Jose Victor Garcia & Jose Julian Espinosa. Middle – Photo of gate at the Garcia Home in Conejos– The Denver Public Library, Western History Collection
Back cover: Garcia House in Conejos circa 1940's

Book Cover – Created by Joe McDaniel - BookCrafters.

Published by Cárcel Publishing
225 West Mangrum Dr.
Pueblo West, Colorado 81007
www.carcelpublishing.com

Publishing assistance by BookCrafters, Parker, Colorado.
www.bookcrafters.net

Dedicated to my parents,
Castelar M Garcia and Anastacia V Garcia

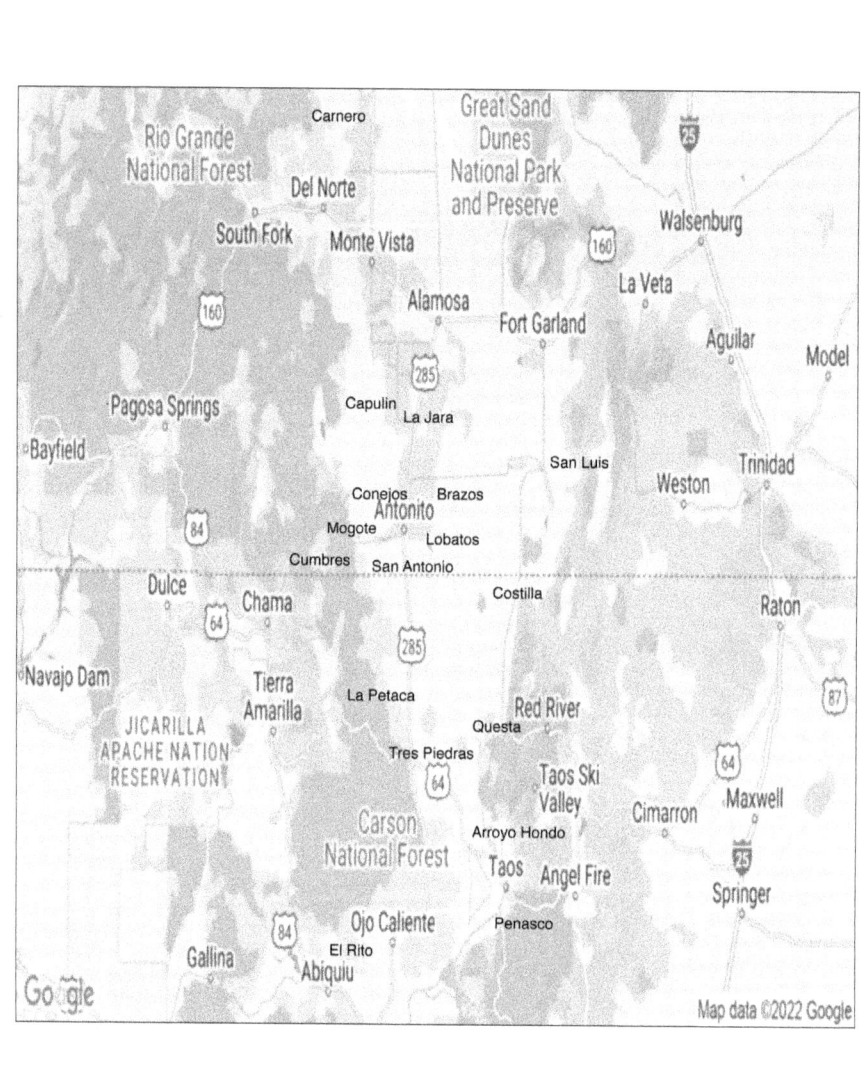

Table of Contents

Acknowledgements

I WAS FORTUNATE TO INHERIT quite a few photographs of our families and my desire has been to share them with my family, extended family, and friends. I have occasionally traveled a distance to get a picture to put them in this book where everyone could see them.

Every weekday morning when I get up to have my coffee and check my email, I have the radio station set to KSTY 104.5 in Canon City, Colorado. I love to listen to them and Ed Norton the station manager. He encourages everyone to write down their family history because if we don't it will be lost. Hopefully we can save some of the family history.

I would like to thank my wife Susanne, my daughter Kristina, and my son Michael for their support in this endeavor. My brothers and sisters, Cas, Kris, Annette, and John were also big supporters.

I took inspiration from Virginia Sanchez, author of *Pleas and Petitions* and *Forgotten Cucharenos of the Lower Valley*, and the amount of research that she did on our history. She provided a whole new perspective on the history of our community.

I want to thank my older, brother, Cas who provided a lot of insight into the family and shared many of the stories about our ancestors. He also provided a number of books and articles that helped me with this project.

I am also very grateful to the following folks for providing some photos that I didn't have and were willing to share them with me.

My sister Kris Espinoza was able to provide some great photos to the Garcia Collection from negatives we found. Whenever I needed assistance with a photo or an article, she was quick to respond and assist me.

I got to spend time with my cousin Gerri Chacon, and she had a wealth of photos from her mother Ellen and her grandmother Candelaria Chacon. We drove to Socorro, New Mexico to meet my cousin Carmel Cortez Garrett who also had a bounty of photos from her grandmother Sofia Cortez. Spending time with cousin Francisco Gallegos also helped to contribute to this book.

I had the opportunity to sit down with my cousin Theresa Topoleski, and she was able to provide some very interesting pictures of Our Lady of Guadalupe Church when it burned down in 1926 along with a host of other photos.

Other cousins who contributed photos were the following:

Eric Cortez
Aglay Garcia
Reggie Garcia
Reyes Garcia
Sandra Gomez
Vicki Graham
Amber Nichols
Charles Trambley
Carmen Ortiz Y Davis
Melissa Espinoza Smart

Contribution of photos to the Valdez and Lopez families came from:

Susanne Garcia
JoAnn Triviso
Diane Martinez

A special thanks goes out to Joe and Jan McDaniel, BookCrafters, for their support and guidance in getting this book published.

And finally, I want to thank the Denver Public Library, Western History Collection for their cooperation on their pictures.

Introduction

IT'S BEEN SAID THAT A PICTURE is worth a thousand words, and I truly believe that. I started on a journey years ago to research my family tree on both sides and also on my wife's. In doing so, wherever I could get pictures of our ancestors I would travel as far as I needed to and as a result, I have accumulated a number of photos of our family. Most of the photos come from my personal collection that I inherited and also family members who have shared their photos. Facebook and Ancestry have also provided a few photos that I use in this book.

My wife Susanne and I retired to Pueblo West, Colorado in 2013 from Indianapolis, Indiana after thirty plus years of working for the United States Department of Defense as a Manager of Software Engineering for the Military Pay System. I enjoy getting up early and get my day going by catching up on correspondence and listening to a local radio station. I have been working on the family history for some time now and realize that the older I get the more difficult it is to remember events and special occasions that happened in the past, much less the information handed down to us by our parents.

My family played an important role in settling of the beautiful San Luis Valley, Conejos County, and the state of Colorado. I would like to share some of the stories and information handed down to me and material that I have acquired through the years. My dad and mom loved to talk about the history of their families. My father was a great source of information when it came to the family. He loved taking out his *Ledger News* albums and sharing them with visitors.

My Mother loved to talk about growing up in Capulin and leaving the house when she was thirteen to go work for a family that produced honey, eventually making her way to the Jenkins where she would work until she met and married my father. My parents were my heroes and I sometimes wish I could go back in time and ask them questions about my ancestors.

In this book I have many heroes and heroines and I attempt to describe them as my parents saw them and how I grew up with them. I realize that I don't have all the history my father or mother did, but I attempt to chronicle it the best I can. My disclaimer is that I am not a historian and quite possibly there might be some error on my part. I hope the person who discovers it would let me know so that I can correct it.

I hope this book on photos of the family will help you to visualize the many individuals who had such a huge impact on our lives. I am going to start the journey with my parents who I owe so much to.

I've also included pages on:

Battle of the Kiowas

Our Lady of Guadalupe Church

Cumbres

The Flood in Conejos

Maria Rosa Villalpando a fifth-generation grandmother.

We also included my wife's side of the family, the Valdez and the Lopez families.

So, with the encouragement of family and friends, I decided to embark on a journey and chronicle the history of the Memories of My Family - Memorias de Mi Familia.

Castelar and Anastasia Garcia

Figure 1 Castelar and Anastasia - Garcia Collection

THIS IS ONE OF MY ALL-TIME FAVORITE pictures of our parents, Medardo Evon Castelar Garcia and Maria Anastacia Vigil. They were well respected and loved in the community.

Castelar M. Garcia

Figure 2 Castelar in his beloved Cumbres - Garcia Collection

Castelar Medardo Evon Garcia was born in Conejos, Colorado on May 19, 1912 and he lived there his whole life.

Figure 3 Castelar & Sevilla - Garcia Collection

Castelar was six years old when his father died and left the ranch to his mother and the family. That is where he pretty much grew up taking care of the land and the animals. He grew to about five feet nine inches and never got to more than one hundred and sixty pounds. He had big hands from all the hard work he did on the ranch. He was very close to his mother and lived with her until he married. His brothers and sisters were older than him, and they would come for dinner at the house with their families and spend time with him and his mother.

When he was a young man, he had an opportunity to travel to California and visit his brothers, Amarante and Julian, along with his sisters Sofia and Sevilla. He tells the story of seeing beach front property in San Clemente for sale for just a few dollars an acre.

He worked the ranch until about 1966 when it was sold, but he also worked as the Deputy County Clerk for Conejos County working for his nephew Reginald Garcia. I had the opportunity to go with him one evening when they were counting the ballots for the general election. It was mostly men back then, and every time a precinct came in with ballots, they would be tabulated and the folks would then talk about the candidate with the most votes. He left working at the Court House and started working to improve his community by getting involved with the Office of Economic Opportunity and a host of community action programs.

He worked closely with Abel Valdez from San Luis on many programs. I remember he would drive to San Luis and on occasion drive over a rattlesnake and put it in the trunk of the car. It was quite discomforting for my mom when she would open the trunk of the car and see a dead reptile. He was involved with the Colorado Congress on Aging and with the help of many of the senior citizens in the Antonito area he started the Antonito Senior Citizen's Center. He was involved with the Volunteers in Service to America (VISTA) and wrote a number of grants to help improve the quality of life for people living in Conejos County.

He enjoyed hunting and the time I enjoyed the most was when he would get up early in the morning, get the coffee going, and then wake me up to go hunting. It would still be dark as we jumped in the truck and headed out to the area we discussed the night before. The places we hunted were Cumbres, Osier, Fox Creek, Sheep Creek, Spruce Hole, Trujillo Meadows, Los Pinos and even the mesa by Manassa. He also enjoyed hunting and fishing with his good friend Adrian Rivera. They would pack their bags for an overnight stay at Adrian's cabin in the Brazos and come home with meat and fish.

He was always the gentleman with our mom and treated her like a lady. He made sure that he walked on the outside of the sidewalk when with her. He loved his children and showed it, although he was not a very emotional person, and he was proud of his children and their accomplishments. He enjoyed sharing his historical insight about the county and loved to talk about his ancestors. He was an active Republican and a Roman Catholic with a deep respect and love for God. He loved to whistle a variety of songs and it was always a treat for me to hear him. A couple of the traits that I share with my dad is that we both love to take naps and eat cookies.

Figure 4 Early photo of Castelar - Garcia Collection

In the background is my Tio Reginaldo with his wife Tia Rosita. The picture was taken in the front lawn of the house in Conejos probably around 1914. I don't know what happened to the tricycle, but I would love to have it today. Dad was just six years old when his father passed away on August 18, 1918, at the age of sixty. Although he didn't get to know his father, he always spoke highly of him and loved to read about him in his beloved *Ledger News*.

*Figure 5 Castelar with his mother, Uncle Galasancio,
brothers, sisters & cousins - Garcia Collection*

Figure 6 Cas holding baby - Garcia Collection

Here is Dad pictured holding a baby. I don't know the name of the little child. Notice the background of the porch around the house and the trees. You can see the barn in the background.

Figure 7 Antonito Jr High School - Garcia Collection

Dad was very fortunate to be able to attend school and the above picture is of him attending Antonito Junior High School in 1926 with his sister Nea being his teacher. My aunt was an amazing woman and I loved stopping by her house whenever I had the opportunity. She was so cordial and welcoming, and I really enjoyed her company. Our dad graduated from Antonito High School in 1930 where he played sports.

Figure 8 Castelar with his brothers and mother - Theresa Topoleski

The above photo shows Julian, Victor, Teodora, amarante and Castelar.

Our father grew up helping on the ranch and learning how to irrigate, put up hay, lambing in the spring, fixing fences, and taking the sheep to the llano and Cumbres. He was responsible for the shearing of the sheep in the spring for the precious wool. In those days homes were warmed during the winter by burning wood. And meals were prepared on a wood burning cook stove with a container on the side that would heat the water. In his home the stove was connected to a water tank to heat water for use in the kitchen and bathroom. He spent time in the fall going to the mountains for wood, he especially liked piñon wood for burning. As a young man he learned to hitch up a team of horses to a wagon and to shoe horses. I was amazed at how he could get those horseshoes to fit so perfectly.

Figure 10 Dad with Cas
- Garcia Collection

Figure 9 Castelar & Anastasia
- Garcia Collection

The above picture is Castelar and Anastasia with Castelar's niece, Geraldine Trambley.

Here is a photo of our father holding our brother Cas in front of his 1930 Model A Ford pickup.

He would often tell us how versatile and useful the little pickup was. It was used for hauling hay, going hunting and getting wood. He would later trade it in for a Willy's Jeep.

Castelar was involved with the Colorado Congress on Aging and was responsible for organizing the Senior Citizen's Center in Antonito. He was the director for many years. The center provided, and probably still does, hot meals at least once a week. They would organize field trips to different parts of the valley and would even head down to New Mexico to gamble at the Indian Reservations. We all used to get a laugh when my dad would talk about the viejitos, and he was one of them. Our dad was also a member of the Antonito Knights of Columbus.

Figure 11 Eloy Martinez and Castelar at the Senior Citizen's Center in Antonito, CO - Garcia Collection

The Antonito Senior Citizen's Center continues to operate to this day. It has been a blessing to many of the Ancianos in the community.

Anastasia Vigil Garcia

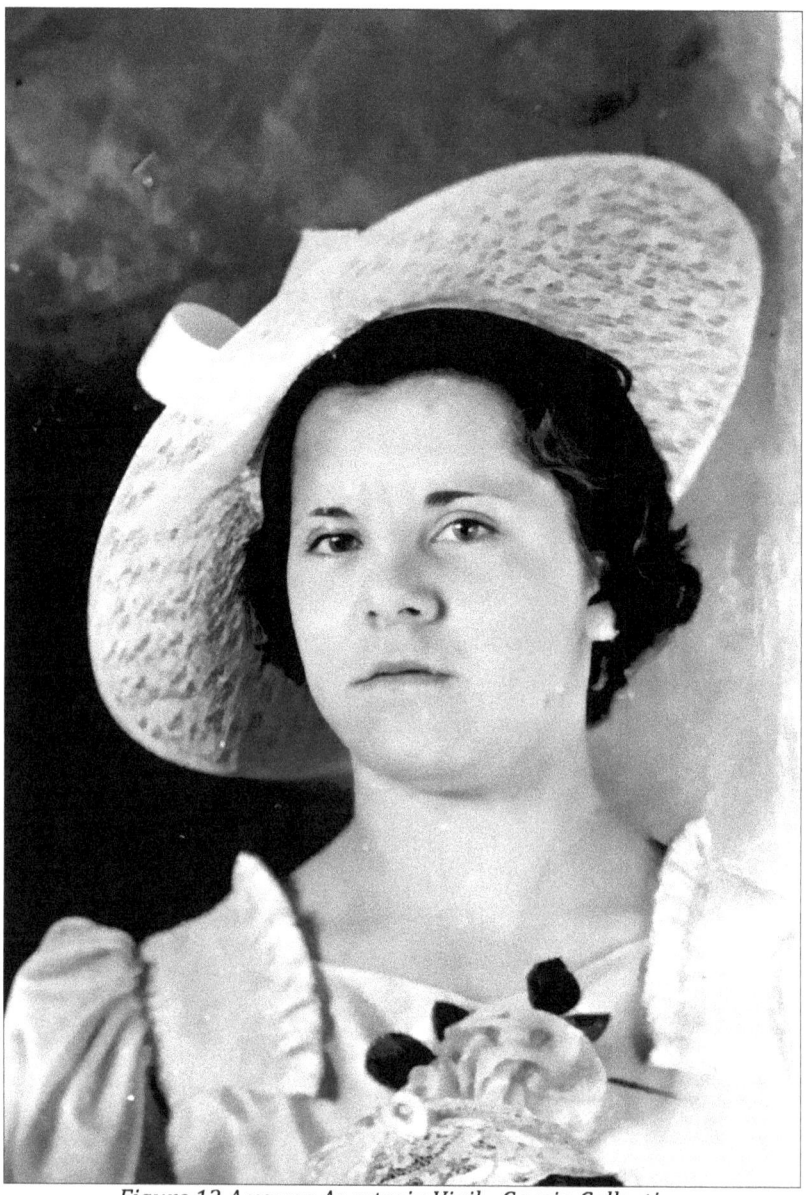

Figure 12 A young Anastasia Vigil - Garcia Collection

ANASTASIA WAS BORN ON FEBRUARY 8, 1919 in the community of Capulin, Colorado. She would walk to school with her brothers and attended until the eighth grade.

At thirteen years of age, she went to work as a live-in house keeper for the Belts who owned a honey farm in La Jara. After a time, she went to work for the Jenkins in Antonito. The Jenkins loved to entertain, and Mom learned a lot from Mrs. Jenkins. Mrs. Jenkins loved to bake and my mom learned to make the best cinnamon rolls ever!

She met my father Castelar, and they went to Las Cruces, New Mexico with his sister Sofia and got married on December

Figure 13 Anastasia - Garcia Collection

24, 1940. After their marriage they moved into Grandmother Teodora's house, and my mom would help grandmother with all the family and friends entertainment plus keep up the house.

Before I was born, we moved into the little four room guest house that was on the property. It had a wood stove for cooking, heating water and warming up the house. There was also a fireplace in the living room. Outside the house we had an outhouse in the chicken coop.

It could be quite an adventure getting through the chickens, especially the rooster, to get to the outhouse. We had one of the few phones in the community and would often get calls for the neighbors. My dad or my brothers would go to the person's home to notify them and bring them to the house so they could get their call. Usually, a call that came at night was because of an emergency in the family.

Mom started working at the Post Office with Consuelo Espinoza. She loved her job because she had the opportunity to visit with all the people from the community. After my two younger siblings, Annette and John were born she made the decision to stay home and raise the kids. When I was born, Consuelo suggested that my middle name be Ronald, hence I became Michael Ronald Garcia. Unfortunately it didn't show up in my birth certificate.

Figure 14 Anastasia at home
- Garcia Collection

Figure 15 Baby Anastasia with her mother Sofia - Garcia Collection

Figure 16 Anastasia, Cas, Castelar & Teodora – Garcia Collection

Our mom was a wonderful cook and baker, and her baked goods were mouth-watering and delicious. She liked to dress up and go out and quite literally would change into a new outfit in a matter of minutes if we were going to take her somewhere. She loved her family and always made us feel so welcome when we visited. There was always a hot meal waiting for you when you got there. She went out of her way for the holidays. The dining room table was extended and the fine China and silverware were set out along with all the serving dishes. Everyone would have a place at the table, however, sometimes the kids had to eat in the kitchen. Most often my Tia Avelina and Tio Pat would be invited to eat with us. Those memories will always hold a special place in our hearts. Following are photos of Castelar and Anastasia's family.

Figure 17 Michael, Annette, John, Kris, Tom and Cas. - Garcia Collection

Figure 18 Kris, Tom, John, Cas, Annette, Mom, Dad and Michael
- Garcia Collection

Figure 19 Uncle Tony, Grandfather Guillermo, Cas, Mom and Tom.
- Garcia Collection

Figure 20 Anastasia with Cas & Uncle Tony
- Garcia Collection

When we were kids, Mom would pack us in the car and we would go looking for quelites (wild spinach) and asparagus that grew alongside the road. And there were the times we would pick chokecherries and champes, and she would make the best jam and jelly.

Mom and Dad liked to go to dances and would travel around the valley to different venues to dance. I had the opportunity to see them dance at an Espinosa family reunion in Albuquerque, and I thought I was watching *Dancing with The Stars*. They were smooth and in sync with each other, and it was exciting to see them glide across the floor.

Having a clean house was important for Mom. Every weekend she would have us cleaning the house and even getting on our knees to dust, wash and wax the floors. Everything had to be dusted.

Mother enjoyed going out. Every time any of us kids would say we are going for a drive, to Taos or some other place, she would go in her bedroom and come out looking like a million dollars.

She enjoyed her plants and flowers. In front of the house we had the lilac bushes, both lavender and white. She loved her hollyhocks next to the kitchen. I remember going out early in the spring mornings and be greeted by the colorful blooming morning glories. Inside she had a Christmas plant that would bloom throughout the year.

Figure 21 Mom and Dad - Garcia Collection

After our father's passing, she stayed all alone in the house where she experienced some interesting ghostly phenomena. She had a lot of friends in town and loved to visit them. She lived by herself for a couple of years and then moved in with Annette and later with Michael and Susanne. We had the opportunity to enroll her in the Total Long Term Care program and she enjoyed going to the senior center and participating in all the activities they had. She would get up early and get ready so she could be on the bus on time. Our mom passed away December 13, 2010.

Our mom and dad celebrated their Fiftieth Anniversary in Cumbres, Colorado. Their wedding was on December 24th but the family decided to have the celebration during the summer so more people could attend. The following page has a couple of pictures of the family during the celebration.

Figure 22 Annette, Cas, Dad, Michael, Mom, John, Kris and Tom
- Garcia Collection

Figure 23 Grandchildren - Back row: Veronica, Dad, Victoria, Mom.
Front row: Michael, Ricky, Timothy & Kristina. Lauren is missing.
- Garcia Collection

Our parents were featured in the December 1, 1996 *Denver Post, Empire Magazine.*

Castelar Garcia and his wife, Anna, at home in Conejos, hold a picture of Castelar's grandfather, Jose Marie Jacques, who helped found the town. Castelar Garcia was born in 1912.

Figure 24 Photo - 1996 Empire Magazine

Jose Victor Garcia

Figure 25 Jose Victor Garcia - Garcia Collection

A BIT HAS BEEN WRITTEN ABOUT MY GREAT-GRANDFATHER Jose Victor Garcia. The pieces of information I gathered from my father and others is that he was a very disciplined and industrious man. He was born on March 6, 1832 in Ranchitos de Ojo Caliente, New Mexico. His Godfather was Cristobal Garcia.

His father was Serafin Garcia who was born March 23, 1799 in Chamita, New Mexico. He was married to Maria De La Luz Aragon, born in 1811 in the New Mexico Territory. Together they had nine children including Jose Victor. Serafin's father was Francisco Xavier Garcia born on May 2, 1762, in San Juan, Rio Arriba New Mexico. He was married to Maria Juana Quintana born on June 28, 1767 in Santa Cruz, New Mexico. Together they had six children.

Maria Juana's great-grandfather was Miguel Matias de Quintana. He was known for having an inquisition put on him by the Catholic Church for some of his writings. By virtue of his ability to understand Canon Law he was exonerated. He would be known as the Mad Poet of New Mexico. There is an excellent book on his life and writings called *Defying the Inquisition in Colonial New Mexico* by Francisco A. Lameli available on Amazon.

According to information I discovered, it seems that Francisco Xavier Garcia died from a lightning bolt. His father Vicente Garcia was born in 1735 in Abiquiu, New Mexico. One bit of information I found mentioned that he was a mulato. He married Maria Juana Trujillo, born on July 15, 1735 in Santa Cruz De La Canada, New Mexico. They were married on January 6, 1757 at the Santo De Tomas Catholic Church in Abiquiu, New Mexico. The information I found on the marriage states they were both Spanish. Together they would have ten children. Vicente is as far back as we can get on the Garcia line, and Maria Juana Trujillo is as far back as we can get on the Trujillo line.

Jose Victor Garcia's early life consisted of hunting buffalo and trading with the local Native Americans. We had his musket at the house for some time, then it went to my brother Tom and now is in possession of his son Ricky. He reached some level of education either by going to school or was self-taught, in either case he was an intelligent individual. Virginia Sanchez, author of *Pleas and Petitions*, available on Amazon, brought up and interesting bit of information concerning our ancestors--many of them learned to speak different Native American languages. Trading with the Native Americans helped them to understand their way of life and the respect they had for the land and animals.

According to the Diary of the Jesuit Residence of Our Lady of Guadalupe

Figure 26 Placida De La Trinidad Silva - Garcia Collection

Parish, Conejos, Colorado, 1871 - 1875, Victor was twenty-two when he fell in love and married Maria Candelaria Jaquez. They were married on November 24, 1854 in Abiquiu, New Mexico. She was the daughter of Jose Maria Jaquez, more about him in a later chapter. Together they would have three children, Jose Alejandro Amarante, Placida and Celestino.

Figure 27 on the following page is of Jose Victor's three children from his first wife, Maria Candelaria Jaquez. Circa 1860's. After his wife's passing in May of 1862, he married Placida De La Trinidad Silva on October 12, 1862 at Our Lady of Guadalupe Church in Conejos. Together they had eleven children. Starting with Maria Isabel, Sevilla, Juan Climaco, Juan Ignacio, Lafayette, Jose Adolfo, Jose Ignacio, Maria Fidela, Maria Delores, Manuel Ignacio and Jose Galasancio.

Jose Victor moved to the San Luis Valley in 1855 with his father-in-law Jose Maria Jaquez, and he would serve as a representative in the New Mexico Territorial Legislature at the age of twenty-seven for two sessions.

By 1861 he was elected to the new Colorado Territorial Legislature representing Conejos along with Jesus Maria Barela from Costilla. Being the only two Hispanics, they fought to have Spanish speaking interpreters at the legislative session and to have the new constitution translated into the Spanish language. My father mentioned a few times to me how Jose Victor was offered property along the Cherry Creek in Denver if he would support voting for the Capitol of Colorado to be in a certain city. My father told me his vote could not be bought. He would vote his conscious.

Figure 27 Jose Amarante, Placida & Celestino - Garcia Collection

Many times, I heard from my father that Jose Victor had petitioned the government to establish the boundary line between Colorado and New Mexico. He also was responsible for getting the San Luis Valley surveyed in 1861. My dad also informed me that his grandfather was opposed to the large land grants that had been given to one individual; he felt that the land should be shared by many instead of just one.

According to my great-grandfather's biography, he acquired a section of land in an area known as Brazos and began ranching after having served in the Colorado Legislature. I've heard stories on how he had to fight off the Native Americans. In 1858 the Utes destroyed

28

his crops and killed his cows, and in 1861 the Arapaho killed his cows and destroyed valuable property. (Interesting that the Arapaho would travel that far west.)

His wife Sofia received a certificate in 1905 (number 7241) for his involvement in the Indian Wars.

Taking the following from his biography, in 1866 he was appointed Collector for Colorado, and in 1872 he was commissioned by then Governor Edward McCook as Brigadier General of the Colorado National Guard, Second Division. A large stone monument honoring his service used to be by his grave in the Conejos Cemetery but someone or somebodies took the monument. In 1874, Governor Samuel E. Elbert appointed him a member of the Board of Managers of the Centennial Exposition in Philadelphia, Pennsylvania. In local affairs he was elected Conejos, County Justice of the Peace in 1857, Conejos County Commissioner in 1884, and General Road Master in 1896.

The *Ledger News* from March of 1899 describes the marriage of his daughter, Dolores to Crescencio DeHerrera. It was the uniting of two very prominent families in the county.

Married.

DeHERRERA—GARCIA — At the Catholic church in onejos at 10 o'clock a. m., Monday February 6, 1899, Crescencio DeHerrera and Miss Doloreas Garcia, Rev. Father Fernandez officiating.

As becomes two of the oldest and most prominent families in the county the affair was grand and elegant, and was attended by a large number of friends. Many more who would have attended were detained at home by the extremely cold weather.

The ceremony, performed by Rev. Father Fernandez, occupied full two hours after which the wedding party and friends departed for the home of the bride's parents Don and Senora Jose V. Garcia, northeast of town, where many more friends were in waiting to receive the party.

A wedding feast was served at about 2 p. m., which was enjoyed by perhaps 100 guests. Later in the evening more young people began to arrive for the merry dance that commenced early in the evening and continued until early morn.

The esteem of many friends was manifested by beautiful and valuable presents.

Mr. and Mrs. DeHerrera left on Wednesday for a short wedding tour to Boulder, where they will visit friends.

The LEDGER unites with their hosts of friends in wishing the happy couple all the joys and success possible in life.

Figure 28 - Garcia Collection

I would like to share another story written in 1898 by the *Ledger News*, titled, "A Serious Accident."

A runaway accident occurred on the street last Saturday that was quite serious in its result and that will probably prompt a revision of the manner in which the town ordinances have been enforced for the last few years.

One of Honorable J.V. Garcia's heavy hay teams was left standing on the street near the depot and became frightened at the rattling of an oil tank and ran away. It circled around the Bardsley block and turned up Main Street which as is customary in our busy town, was thoroughly lined with teams. As it arrived in front of the Ledger office door it overtook Koch & Sampson's delivery wagon which was driven by C.B. Sampson. The horses were large, and as they straddled one on each side of the light delivery wagon, they crushed it to the ground. The end of the pole struck Mr. Sampson in the back of the head and knocked him to the ground while his horse was also overcome by the big team and went down. Mr. Sampson fell against his horse and landed on the ground out of the way of the wreck, except one leg which was run over by the front wheel of the hay wagon. He was carried into Emil Koch's room where Drs. Johnson and Lawson looked after his injuries, which consists of an ugly scalp wound, an injured leg and several minor bruises, none of which proved nearly so serious as was at first feared, though they were very sore and troublesome for some days. A carriage containing a ranchman and family barely escaped the wreck by driving across the sidewalk. While Mr. Sampson is right in his opinion that the wreck was serious enough, the result would have been fearful in comparison had the runaway horse struck the covered carriage containing the ranchman and family.

Mr. Garcia did the very commendable thing by

directing the doctors to send their bills to him and
also by directing W. D. Carroll to deliver a new wagon
to Koch & Sampson.

Jose Victor died on September 10, 1900 at his home in Brazos with his family by his side. He was sixty-eight at the time of his passing. From what I read he had one of the largest funerals in the county and was buried at the cemetery in Conejos. I often think of him and the struggles that he faced and the adjustments he had to make when the property that he lived on went from a New Mexico territory with all its laws and customs done in the New Mexico tradition to the Colorado Territory with new laws and regulations written in English.

I believe the photo below are the daughters of Jose Victor, Maria Fidela and Maria Dolores. Both were married into the DeHerrera family. If there is a family member who could identify them, I would be most grateful.

I took the next photo (Figure 30) when I was researching the Captive Indians Report and posted it to Facebook. This report was produced by the Indian Agent for the U. S. Government, Lafayette Head in 1865.

Most notably you will see Jose Victor's name on the first page. But if you look closely, you will also see his father-in-law's name of Jose Maria Jaquez on this page. On the third page not listed here is his father Serafin Garcia. My great-grandfather, Jose Julian Espinosa also had acquired Indians.

Interesting to note is that Lafayette Head did not list himself or any of the other Anglos in the report.

Figure 29 Garcia Sisters - Garcia Collection

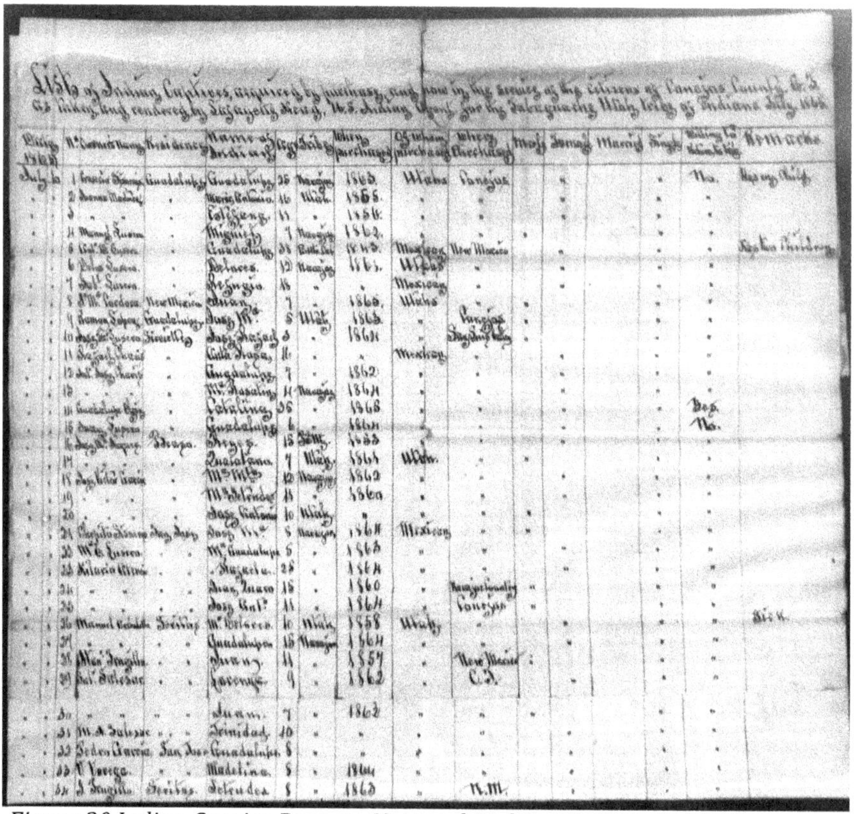

Figure 30 Indian Captive Report - National Archives & Records Administration

My personal belief is that Jose Victor, along with a number of leading Hispanic members of the community, filed a complaint about the fact that he was not properly distributing the goods and supplies that were supposed to go to the Indians. For more information on this subject, I would suggest that you read *Pleas and Petitions* by Virginia Sanchez available on Amazon.

What I have been able to gather on our family about the Indian captives was that some were used as servants and others were baptized and adopted into the family. In the baptismal records from Our Lady of Guadalupe on January 24, 1861, we find Jose Antonio, an eight-year-old Indian being baptized, but also stating that he was adopted by Jose Victor Garcia and Maria Candelaria Jaquez. And in December of 1861 there is a record of Maria Gertrudis being baptized and raised by Jose Victor and Maria Candelaria. On June 30, 1864

Maria Antonia was baptized and she was raised by Jose Victor and his second wife Placida De Silva.

In the book *Forgotten Cucharenos of the Lower Valley*, written by Virginia Sanchez and available on Amazon, she mentions that after the 1866 Civil Rights Act was passed, my great-grandfather, Jose Julian Espinosa was accused by some members of the New Mexico Territorial District Court to be holding captives. It was eventually dismissed. He and his wife did raise a young Ute Indian named Justo and integrated him into their family.

In the 1870 Census, Jose Maria Jaquez is in Huerfano County and has his grandchildren, Placida and Celestino with him, but an Indian by the name of Cayetano was also there. I suspect he was sent to watch over the children.

One has to remember that our ancestors traded and did business with the Native Americans, and people were bought and sold within the Indian community. One of my fifth great-grandmothers, Rosa Maria Villalpando was one such person who was captured and sold. More on her later in the book.

Figure 31 Jose Victor & Placida Trinidad final resting place
- Garcia Collection

Previous page is a photo of the gravestones of Jose Victor Garcia and his wife Placida Trinidad Silva. Unfortunately, the monument built to honor him for his service as the first Brigadier General of the Colorado Militia was stolen.

The Battle of the Kiowas and Utes

THERE ARE DIFFERENT STORIES as to what took place here, so I will give a *Reader's Digest* version. In 1859 the area known as Cerritos was settled by a well-respected man known as Tata Atanasio Trujillo, whom Trujillo Meadows was named after. A band of Kiowa intended to inflict harm on the Utes who were encamped not too far away from this place. The Utes found out and assembled a war party and chased the Kiowa to this area and surrounded them.

The Kiowa put up a barrier with stones around themselves and after a day of battling each other, one Ute brave was able to penetrate the makeshift fortress and all the Kiowa were eventually killed. Upon finding out what took place and smelling the stench coming from the dead bodies, Atanasio Trujillo requested that Jose Victor Garcia, Celedon Valdez, Ignacio Trujillo and a few others bury the bodies. Depending on the story, the body count could have been as low as just a handful or as many as sixty to two hundred.

Figure 32 Cerrito De Los Kiowas

Jose Victor Garcia

Born 1832, County of Taos, New Mexico
Died 1918 1900
Dates served in Colorado Legislature:
1861-1864 Territorial Council
1867-1868 Territorial Council
1872-1874 Territorial Council

Jose Victor Garcia served as a Republican in the Territorial House from 1861 to 1864 as well as in the Territorial Council from 1872 to 1874, representing both Conejos and Costilla Counties. Interestingly, though a lifelong Republican, he also served as a Democrat from Conejos County from 1867-1868 in the Territorial House. Additionally, he served in the territorial legislature of New Mexico in 1859-1860, prior to the firm establishment of territorial lines between the two future states. In 1872, Governor McCook commissioned him as a brigadier-general of the Colorado National Guard, second division—the first Hispanic to take such a position in the state.

Mr. Garcia is considered one of the pioneers of Conejos County. He was born in 1832 in New Mexico, just forty miles north of Santa Fe, and traced his lineage to early Spanish settlers there. At the age of twenty-eight, he began to trade with Apache, Navajo and Ute Indians—a business he continued for seven years. Indeed, his familiarity with Indians at a young age may have been invaluable, as he and his family struggled to control a ranch of some 940 acres. Reports of his time indicate that early settlers faced significant peril. A biography written on Jose Victor Garcia found in the Walsenburg Library notes: "Indians were very troublesome. In 1858 the Utes destroyed his crops and killed five of his cows, while three years afterward the Arapahos killed thirteen of his cows; and at other times they destroyed other stock and valuable property." Strangely enough, he is mentioned in Major Lafayette Head's List of Indian Captives as having purchased three Indians: Maria Gertrudis, a Navajo, Maria also a Navajo and Jose Antonio, a Ute.

Mr. Garcia made a living ranching on the Conejos River, where he took a squatter's claim on a section of government land. He was the first individual to appeal to the national government to have the San Luis Valley surveyed, which was done in 1861, and he appealed to Governor Gilpin in 1862 to have the line between New Mexico and Colorado firmly established. Among other roles, Jose Victor Garcia also served his community as justice of the peace and commissioner and inspector of roads for Conejos County.

Figure 33 Jose Victor Garcia – Courtesy of Gerri Chacon

35

Celestino Garcia

CELESTINO WAS BORN ON DECEMBER 8, 1861 in Conejos. His mother, Maria Candelaria Jaquez passed away six months later in May of 1862. Like his father, Jose Victor, Celestino would take up ranching and also serve in the Colorado General Assembly. He served for a number of years and eventually retired from political office to focus on his ranch. His first marriage was to Mary Rose Garcia, and they had two daughters. His second marriage was to Sidelia Trujillo, and they had nine children all of which received an education.

Figure 34 Jose Celestino Garcia
- Garcia Collection

One of his sons, Labre, upon his retirement from the U.S. Government, came to visit my father at the house in Conejos one day, and I happened to be there. He lived in Washington D.C. and immediately you could tell he had done well in life and was very well educated. Whenever my father would speak to him in Spanish he could not answer. My father was taken back a bit and told me later that people should not forget their heritage and language, something that I have carried with me to this day. All in all, we had a great visit with him as he was very interested in the family history. As a side note, a potato barn on the property that Celestino owned has been entered into the National Register of Historic Places by my cousin, Dr. Reyes Garcia.

Celestino Jose Garcia

Born 1861, Conejos County, Colorado
Dates served in Colorado Legislature:
1893-1911 House
1915-1919 House

Celestino Garcia was a native Coloradan, growing up and spending most of his life in Conejos County. He was the third of eleven children in the family of Jose Victor Garcia. Educated in the English and Spanish schools of Conejos, Mr. Garcia was fully versed in both languages, enabling him to serve his community in a variety of posts throughout his life. (He acted as an interpreter for the Conejos County Commissioners from 1886 to 1892, an interpreter in the Senate in 1885, and an interpreter in the House in 1887.) He finished his schooling at the Jesuit College in Pueblo under Father Pinto, an early Colorado pioneer. Upon completion of his studies he moved to Alamosa, where he worked as a clerk for over ten years before returning to the livestock industry near Antonito. Being reared on the rough frontier, Mr. Garcia became familiar early in life with the particular needs and characteristics of his district. This fact coupled with the esteemed position of his father in state and local politics helped to launch the young man on his own career.

He commenced his political career as a page in the First General Assembly and held office almost continuously from that time through 1919. He was elected to the Ninth and Tenth General Assemblies as a Democrat and enjoyed the endorsement of all other parties. He returned to the Eleventh, Twelfth, Thirteenth and Fourteenth Assemblies as a Republican nominee and again received the endorsement of all other parties. As noted in the *Official Roster of the Fourteenth General Assembly of Colorado*, published in 1903:

Mr. Garcia holds his seat in the legislature more by appointment than election as he is the unanimous choice of the people regard-less of party affiliation; never, but one time has he received a dissenting vote. As a legislator he is aggressive and alert that no move of the opponent escapes him. Of strong personality, well grounded in parliamentary tactics he is thoroughly qualified to wield the gavel. He is one of the most influential members and that his ability and good judgment are recognized is evidenced by him being placed on the most important committees.

Mr. Garcia wielded much influence as chairman of the railroads and corporations and judiciary committees, among other appointments. He went on to serve as a Democrat and as a Republican in the House from 1915 to 1919 representing Conejos County, rounding out a career of twenty-two years in the Colorado General Assembly.

7

Figure 35 Celestino Jose Garcia - Garcia Collection

37

Maria Placida Delfina Garcia Cantu

I FOUND THE BELOW PHOTO in Ancestry, and it is difficult to determine who posted the photo. It was primarily for Jose Candido Cantu, but I believe the woman is Maria Placida Delfina Garcia, she bears a resemblance to her brothers. She was born on December 28, 1859 in Conejos to Jose Victor Garcia and Maria Candelaria Jaquez. She has the distinction of being one of the first to be registered in Our Lady of Guadalupe baptismal records for Conejos, Colorado. She was married to Patricio Trujillo on January 25, 1875 at her father's ranch and they had three children: Maria Candelaria, Virginia and Ignacio. Her husband died at the age of thirty. She then met and married Jose Candido Cantu and it seems that they had one child by the name of Placida. He was appointed Postmaster of the post office in Los Cerritos, Colorado in 1899 and represented Conejos County in the Colorado House of Representatives between 1911 and 1914. After Placida's death he married Maria Eva Sisneros.

Figure 36 Jose Candido Cantu & Placida - Ancestry

Jose Amarante Garcia

ALTHOUGH I NEVER GOT TO MEET my grandfather, he died thirty-five years before I was born, he is a larger-than-life person in my world.

Figure 37 Jose Amarante Garcia – Garcia Collection

My grandfather was born on June 1, 1858, probably in the area known as the Brazo where my grandfather had acquired property. He was baptized June 10th by Father Montano at a chapel that had been built on the property of his padrinos, Celedon and Maria Guadalupe Valdez making him one of the first persons to be baptized into the Catholic Church in Colorado.

Dad would often tell us about the education his father received and that he even lived with Senator George M Chilcott for a bit. In 1869-70 he attended the public schools of Pueblo and in 1871 he attended school in Denver. In 1873 at the age of 15 he was elected interpreter of the House of Representatives. In 1877 he was elected to the same position in the State Senate. I believe the Hispanic Representatives needed a reliable interpreter and he most certainly fit the bill. While in Denver he became known as Joseph Garcia. His ability to speak two languages would serve him well both in the political arena as well as in business. In 1881 he was elected to represent Conejos and Costilla counties in the House of Representatives.

In 1887 he was elected sheriff of Conejos County and served in that capacity for nineteen consecutive years by re-election.

Dad told me about his ability to track a person while riding a horse, and his skill with a pistol was unmatched. His reputation as a sheriff was known throughout the United States. For many years it was an admitted impossibility for a criminal to escape from the San Luis Valley which has a mountain contour of more than 300 miles.

Back volumes of the *Antonito Ledger News* contain various accounts of his adventures with the hardest criminals of the country. He subdued many heavy crimes by his official skill and held petty offenders under subjection to a noticeable degree by occasionally inflicting summery punishment upon a degenerate. He justified that action by saying nothing was accomplished by hauling such an offender through

Figure 38 Jose Amarante Garcia - Garcia Collection

the court, and the expense to lay out in a fine in jail where he would take life easy for the time and then return to repeat the same offense. While these acts were not always sustained by law, the undercurrent of public opinion seemed to have generally approved.

During his career he killed two men for which he was exonerated by the courts. He performed the last official public hanging in Colorado which was held behind the jail in Conejos, Colorado on July 16, 1889. After this hanging all hangings took place inside the Colorado State Penitentiary.

In the photo below my grandfather is the person on the left reading Mr. Jose Abram Ortiz his sentence. Mr. Ortiz killed a man for his shoes. Father Tomassini said a prayer with him and Mr. Eels the deputy sheriff pulled the lever to drop Mr. Ortiz. It was said by my grandmother that after the hanging, he came home and threw up.

Figure 39 Last official hanging in Colorado
- The Denver Public Library, Western History Collection

Jose Amarante Garcia served as sheriff for Conejos County from 1887 until 1906. He then went into private business. From papers we found in the house, he did a lot of real estate transactions all over the Valley. In 1912 he was elected County Judge and served in that capacity until his death in August of 1918. He was also involved with ranching and had amassed quite a number of sheep and cattle. He took the sheep to Chama and leased land from the Tierra Amarilla Land Grant.

I heard the story of how my grandfather had a woman who watched him when he was growing up, and he became very attached to her. Her name was Mrs. Andrea Martinez, and her family had been friends of the Garcia's for many years. At an advanced age she was caught selling alcohol to the Indians in Ignacio and was given a six-month sentence to be served in Pueblo County Jail.

Once my grandfather heard about it, he immediately went to Pueblo armed with a release from the Denver Federal Court Judge R. E. Lewis and was able to obtain her freedom. He then took her back to Ignacio under his care. He could not picture a 75-year-old feeble Castilian woman spending time in a jail, especially one who's family had done so much for him.

The photos next page show Jose Amarante entertaining the County Clerk, Mr. H. Russell along with his family. According to the family history, the home in Conejos was originally a trading post. I

McNEEL,   Conejos, Colo

Figure 40 Jose Amarante Garcia
- Garcia Collection

recall my father saying that Native Americans had been killed in front of the trading post. That probably explains the sound of voices we've heard in the evening while approaching the house when there was no one around.

Figure 41 House in Conejos - Garcia Collection

Figure 42 House in Conejos - Garcia Collection

A Mr. Charles Brickenstein, who was the County Treasurer for a period of seventeen years, built this magnificent home in 1880. The original walls were made of adobe, and they were very wide.

Sheriff J. A. Garcia has reconsidered his plans to build a house on his ranch as noted in these columns last week and purchased the Brickenstein property in Conejos. It would require several years to accomplish such improvement on the ranch as Mr. Garcia has been able to purchase. There are probably no premises in Conejos county more beautiful and picturesque than Mr. Garcia's purchase.

Figure 43 Ledger News May 19, 1906 - Garcia Collection

Figure 44 Photo of Conejos House - Garcia Collection

Jose Amarante was going to build a home on his ranch and already had the plans when Mr. Charles Brickenstein lost over $60,000 of the county's money he had deposited in The Bank of Alamosa which failed in 1906. He resigned his office as County Treasurer after seventeen years of service in March and sold his home to my grandfather. My father told me that he had purchased the home in May of 1906 for ten thousand dollars. The jail was already there when he purchased it. We believe the jail to have been a territorial jail and the first one in the state of Colorado.

Our grandfather enjoyed reading and learning. In fact, he owned the complete set of the 1909 *Harvard Classics*. It was said that if you read the complete set of thirty-eight volumes, you would have earned the equivalent of a Bachelor's Degree from a respected college.

There was a lot of entertaining at the Garcia home. It had a formal entry and a elegant dining room with a large oak dining table that would expand, and it was accompanied by a large number of matching chairs. Plus, there was a fireplace to keep the area warm and inviting. There was also a comfortable living room to host guests.

He was married to his first wife, Sofia Amada Espinosa, (Figure 46) the daughter of Captain Jose Julian Espinosa, on July 25, 1881 at the Carnero Catholic Church in Saguache County. My understanding is that

it was a lavish wedding and Lafayette Head and his wife Martina were the witnesses.

Our grandfather was also a member of the Oddfellows Lodge in Antonito. In addition he was a member of La Sociedad Proteccion Mutua De Trabajadores Unidos (SPMDTU) and was a featured speaker at one of their 4th of July events circa 1900.

Figure 45 Jose Amarante with his two brothers, Ignacio & Celestino - Garcia Collection

A couple of news articles that I have on Jose Amarante, one is when he went to New York City to bring back Abraham Schiffer to the county to pay for his crime. Mr. Schiffer had embezzled a lot of money from the Alamosa Bank and fled to New York to be with his brother who was a millionaire. He was apprehended by local authorities and it was Jose Amarante's duty to go to New York and bring him back. Evidently, our grandfather's reputation preceded him because when he got to New York city, the local media was all impressed with his western appearance, how well-spoken he was and how he carried himself with dignity and confidence.

The second article described his ability to shoot his Colt 44 long barrel pistol. It was mentioned in the paper that at one hundred and fifty yards he could send a bullet through an ordinary playing card about five times out of five.

Figure 46 Jose Amarante with his first wife, Sofia - Garcia Collection

Figure 47 is Jose Amarante with Sofia and their family. Bottom row is Reginaldo, Julianita, Alejandro and the baby is Rufina. On the back row is Irinea, his wife Sofia, Candelaria, and Jose Amarante holding the baby Rufina. All the children were well dressed and well mannered.

Figure 47 Family with Sofia - Courtesy of Gerri Chacon

Figure 48 is a picture that my cousin Gerri Chacon shared with me of Sofia and her two girls. Irinea on the left died at the age of thirteen and Julianita passed away at seven and a half.

Figure 48 Sofia with her daughters, Irinea & Julianita
- Courtesy of Gerri Chacon

Before his wife died, my grandfather tried everything to get her well, even going to Ojo Caliente with the hope that she would get better. She passed away from tuberculosis on June 25, 1898. He then married her sister, our grandmother, Maria Teodora Espinosa on August 4, 1898, at the church in Carnero. It was a small celebration with just the family attending.

*Figure 49 Jose Amarante and Teodora Espinosa
on their wedding day - Garcia Collection*

Figure 50 Jose Amarante and Teodora
- Courtesy of Carmel Cortez Garrett

A photo shortly after their wedding.

Figure 51 Jose Amarante and Teodora with their blended family
– Garcia Collection

Jose Amarante's blended family with children from the first marriage and with our grandmother, Teodora. Bottom row; Victor, Sofia, Julian, Erinea and Amarante. Middle row; Candelaria, Jose Amarante holding Avelina and Teodora. Top row; Placida, Reginaldo and Rufina. Missing is my father, Castelar and my aunt Sevilla. I believe this photo was taken in 1912, the year my father was born. Three other children died at birth or within a year: Julian who died shortly after being born in 1907, Teodorita Serafina lived about a year and half and passed away in 1916, and Angelito who died a few days after being born.

Figure 52 Jose Amarante Garcia and Teodora family
- Garcia Collection

Bottom row; Irinea and Amarante. Middle row; Victor, Jose Amarante, Teodora holding Julian and Sofia. Back row; Placida and our great-grandfather, Captain Jose Julian Espinosa. Photo was taken around 1909.

There are stories of him using tact or diplomacy to apprehend criminals and sometimes force. He would be accused of being too harsh on criminals and probably in today's environment he would not have gotten away with it. Yet he had compassion for the day-to-day worker. Once, while on a train going to Denver, he spotted some Hispanic men who had to work on the railroad with very poor equipment. He made the conductor stop the train and told the foreman to go and get the proper tools for the men. Only after the men had received their tools did the train commence running again.

Another story on his marksmanship came from my father. He told me about his trip to New York City to bring back a criminal named Mr. Schiffer. Somehow the media got wind of his ability to shoot his Colt 44 pistol and they wanted to see a demonstration. They were by a river and there was a bird sitting on a branch across from the river. Without a bit of hesitation, he drew his pistol and quickly shot the bird. All were amazed by his ability.

Figure 53 Jose Amarante with other Sheriffs. He is in the middle with his hands crossed. - Garcia Collection

Figure 54 Ledger News - Garcia Collection

He believed in education and was continually educating himself. He made sure that there were books in the house for his children to read and learn. All of his children went to school and graduated from high school, which was quite an accomplishment in those days, with many going on to college. He was especially proud to see his daughters go to college and become teachers, nurses, get involved in business, and one of his daughters went on to become a Nun in the Catholic Church.

Jose Amarante Garcia died on August 18, 1918 after suffering from a long illness. His funeral was one of the largest that the county had ever witnessed. His casket was kept in the home during the wake. According to the article written about him he left behind quite an estate.

Every Memorial Day our father would take his rake and shovel and go to the cemetery to clean up his father's and grandfather's graves.

His first wife Sofia is buried in this same plot. Due to flooding our grandmother, Teodora was buried in Alamosa.

Figure 55 Coffin in the Garcia home living room - Garcia Collection

Figure 56 Jose Amarante's final resting place near to his father.
- Garcia Collection

*Figure 57 Jail window
- Garcia Collection*

*Figure 58 Jail door
- Garcia Collection*

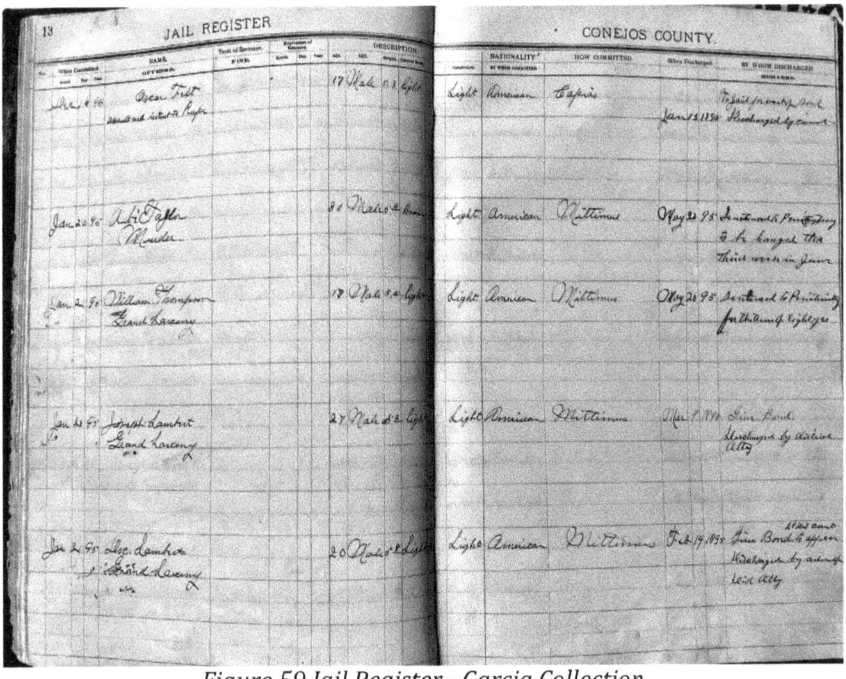

Figure 59 Jail Register - Garcia Collection

Previous page Figure 59 from the register is dated 1895 and it has a Mr. Taylor going to the penitentiary to be hanged for murder. All hangings after the Ortiz hanging were done at the Colorado State Penitentiary.

I was told that when he saw this political ad he laughed all day long.

THE MODERN NAPOLEON

Figure 60 Political Ad - Garcia Collection

Teodora Espinosa Garcia

Figure 61 Teodora Espinosa Garcia - Garcia Collection

OUR GRANDMOTHER WAS TWENTY YEARS OLD when she married Jose Amarante and took on the responsibility of raising her sister's children and starting a family of her own.

Figure 62 Teodora - Courtesy of Carmel Cortez Garrett

Together with her husband, she had eleven children of which three passed away either at birth or within the year.

After her husband passed away, she had the responsibility of raising her children and taking care of the ranch and other properties that grandfather left her. Going through some of the paperwork at the house we found a number of receipts where she sold wool to pay off debts.

Grandmother Teodora with her family according to their birth dates from oldest to youngest. Picture was probably taken mid 1920's. Left to right: Grandmother, Sofia, Victor, Nea, Amarante, Julian, Avelina, Castelar and Sevilla. She was married for twenty years and was forty years old when her husband passed away. She never remarried. Her family always came first in her life.

She was always willing to lend a hand. When the Church burned down in 1926, she helped feed the workers.

She also belonged to the Christian Mothers of Conejos, a society established in 1880 by Our Lady of Guadalupe Church in Conejos.

Figure 63 Teodora with her family - Courtesy Theresa Topoleski

Oldest Parish Society Members

The oldest members of what is probably the oldest parish society in the state of Colorado are these members of the Christian Mothers of Conejos. The society had its beginning Jan. 25, 1880, in Our Lady of Guadalupe church, Conejos, which is the oldest formally established parish in the state, dating back to 1859.

Mrs. Librada Ruperta Lopez (top left) is a charter member of the society and the only one of the founders still living. She the oldest member of any Catholic society in Colorado. Mrs. Beatriz Garcia (top center) became a member of the organization June 6, 1881, and still does her share in caring for the sanctuary of the church in Conejos. Mrs. Sofia L. De Herrera (top right) was enrolled Jan. 25, 1893. Mrs. Fedelina Martinez (bottom left) joined March 27, 1896. Mrs. Ines Galvez (bottom center) became a member Sept. 25, 1898; and Mrs. Teodora Garci

Figure 64 Christian Mothers of Conejos
- Southern Colorado Register

Top row is Mrs. Librada Ruperta Lopez, Mrs. Beatriz Garcia, and Mrs. Sofia L. De Herrera. Bottom row is Mrs. Fedelina Martinez, Mrs. Ines Galvez and Teodora Garcia with her grandson Charles Trambley II.

Dad would mention that his mother had beautiful skin because she would wash her face with cold water every morning. He also told the story of an owl that harassed the chickens and small animals around the house and how his mother came out of the house with a rifle and with one shot did away with the owl.

Grandmother passed away on July 1, 1957 at the nursing home in Del Norte, Colorado and was buried in the cemetery in Alamosa.

Figure 65 Teodora - Garcia Collection

Jose Maria Jaquez

JOSE MARIA JAQUEZ was our great-great-grandfather on my dad's side of the family. I find this relative to be very interesting and I hope to share some insights into his life. He was born April 25, 1819, in San Juan Pueblo in the Territory of New Mexico. His wife was Maria Yrinea Vigil who was born on July 8, 1823, in Rio Arriba, New Mexico and they were married about 1843. Together they had a daughter Maria Candelaria, a son Ramon and an adopted Ute Indian girl Maria De Los Reyes. His father was Felipe De Jesus the first, and he was born on March 20, 1789, in San Juan de Los Caballeros, New Mexico. His mother was Maria Micaela Chaves born on September 26, 1796 in Sandia, New Mexico. Together, Felipe and his wife Maria had nine children starting with Maria Manuela, Jose Maria, Maria Encarnacion, Maria Josefa, Maria Deluvina, Maria Vicenta, Juan Bautista, Maria Augustina, and Maria Gertrudis.

Figure 66 Jose Maria Jaquez - Meliton Velasquez

Felipe De Jesus and his wife followed their son to the new frontier of the San Luis Valley. He passed away October 10, 1863 and was buried in the Church in Conejos. He was buried in the first section that according to records cost $25 for the plot and $100 to the priest. Evidently, the closer you got to the altar the more expensive it was.

Figure 67 Our Lady of Guadalupe 1874-Wheeler Expedtion
– The Denver Public Library, Western

The old Catholic church at Conejos is to be heated by a furnace. C. A. Moore is now excavating a cellar, where the furnace will be located. After the excavating was begun it was discovered that in the early days the place was used for a cemetery. The remains of several skeletons were uncovered. But little remained of the forms except the larger bones of the arms and legs. One body had evidently been buried with its boots on. A pair of expensive knee boots which could possibly have been placed upon a body after death were unearthed. The bones dug up were carefully interred in another place.

Figure 68 Ledger News 1905 - Garcia Collection

According to census records, Jose Maria was well able to pay for his father's burial in the church. By virtue of Felipe De Jesus the first coming to Colorado and being buried here it makes my brothers, sisters, and myself sixth generation Coloradoans.

Felipe's father was Jose Julian Jaquez, and he was born in 1758, on the Villalpando Estancia near Taos, New Mexico. His mother was Maria Paula Martin, born on January 26, 1766 in Rio Arriba, New Mexico. Jose and his wife Paula had nine children, starting with Juan Manuel, Maria Gertrudis, Juan de Jesus, Felipe de Jesus I, Maria Manuela, Maria Pacifica, Manuel Benancio, Felipe de Jesus II and Maria Ysabel. Jose Julian's father was Juan Jose, and he was born on February 15, 1725 in Guadalupe de El Paso Del Norte, New Mexico.

His mother was Maria Rosa Villalpando born on October 12, 1738, in San Juan New Mexico. The estancia where he was born was raided by the Comanches in the summer of 1760, and his father was killed and his mother taken captive. We'll discuss Maria Rosa in a later chapter. We don't know who raised him but when he had grown and married, he spent a great deal of time drinking and in general being a nuisance.

Jose Maria not only had his father who was named Felipe De Jesus, but he also had an uncle named Felipe De Jesus, only he was the second. His descendants would settle in San Luis. Nora Jacquez wrote an interesting book on Jose Eusequio Jacquez, a prominent citizen of San Luis and who was a son of Felipe the Second. Jose Eusequio had two wives and thus two families who were very successful and important in the growth and prosperity of the town of San Luis.

Jose Maria Jaquez, at an early age was named one of thirty-six grantees on the La Petaca Land Grant that consisted of 187,000 acres near Tres Piedras, New Mexico. On August 25, 1892 he turned over his deed of the land grant to his grandson, Jose Amarante Garcia which turned out to be about five thousand acres. I was told that the family had gone to take a look at the property and were not very thrilled with it. Considering that they had beautiful hay fields in the valley and lush green pasture in the majestic San Juan Mountains. I don't know if he sold it or just let it go.

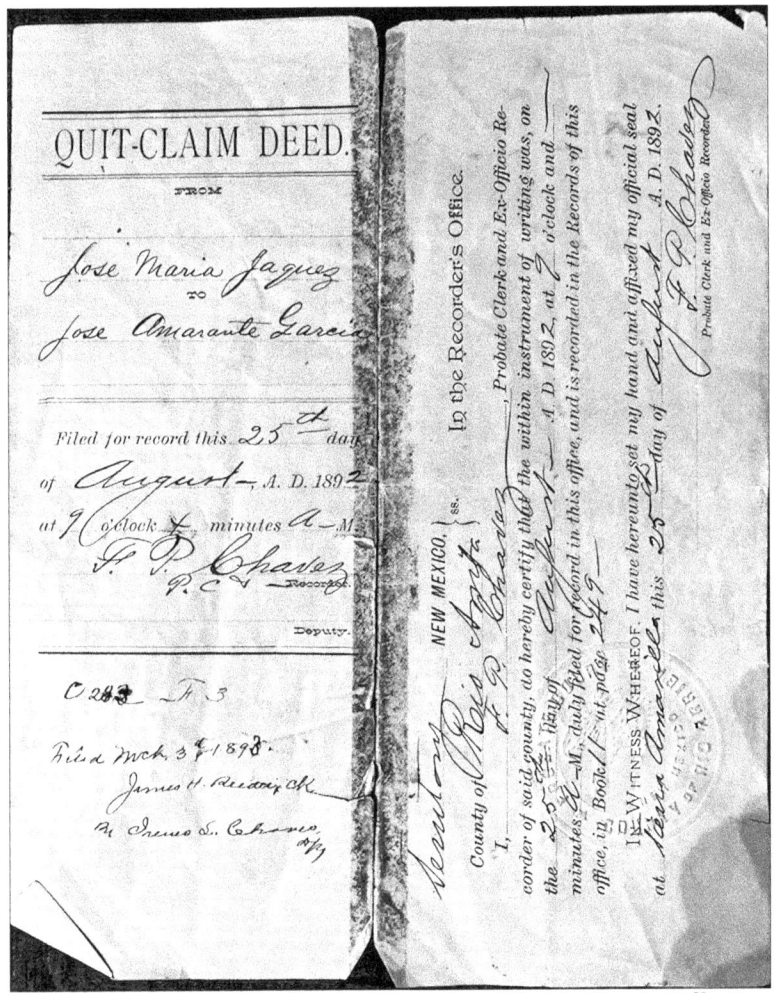

Figure 69 Quit Claim Deed on La Petaca Land Grant - Garcia Collection

Our father would often tell us that it was his grandfather, Jose Maria Jaquez who brought the early settlers into the Valley and not Lafayette Head as many supposed. He was instrumental in bringing a group of settlers in 1854 to the Guadalupe area and would return again in 1855 with more people along with Lafayette Head. He was quite an industrious individual and I don't know how he learned about milling or distilling but when he brought the settlers into the Valley, he built a mill and a distillery. Folks from all over the valley would come to the mill to get their grains milled and at the same time get some liquor. My cousin Gerri Chacon has one of the original mill stones.

Battle of Guadalupe/Conejos

FROM SOME NOTES THAT I FOUND, one morning in March of 1855, the new settlers woke up to find that they had been surrounded by Indians and their livestock was being taken away. They gathered what guns they had and fought off the warriors and attempted to recover their livestock. I've not found any records to indicate if lives were lost.

I don't know where he received his education or if he ever went to school, but he must have been a very intelligent and talented person. The 1885 Census finds him in Huerfano County, and they list his occupation as a musician.

Figure70 Mill stone
- Gerri Chacon

In 1860 he was a member of the Colorado Militia serving as a Lieutenant and from what I've read about him, he must have been a man of means. One tax assessment form I found lists him as having a carriage, not a wagon, but a carriage along with cattle and sheep.

I've tried to locate his burial place to no avail. What I did find is that he was living in Conejos County in the 1860 Census, but the 1870 Census we find him in Huerfano County. His grandchildren from his daughter Maria Candelaria, Placida and Celestino, plus an Indian servant by the name of Cayetano were with him and his wife. From what I can gather, his daughter passed away in 1862, and an Indian daughter Maria De Los Reyes whom he and his wife had purchased from the Mexicans, according to Lafayette Head's report, and whom they raised, married a Jose Morales and moved to Huerfano.

While living in Badito, his wife Yrinea passed away and he married a Maria Antonia Valdez in 1874 in Costilla, and she died in 1879. In 1880 he married, Juana Maria Sanchez and from the census report in 1885 they had a daughter named Liberata born July 31, 1881. Another female is listed but I can't determine what happened to her.

Liberata married a man by the name of Epifanio Ortiz on January 9, 1897 in Antonito, Colorado. Father Tomassini was the officiant and my grandfather, Jose Amarante along with his wife, Sofia were the witnesses. Liberata and Epifanio had seven children; Julius, Natividad, Louis Jerry, Salina Sally Madeline, Epifanio Jr, Annie and Alfonso. She passed away August 25, 1945 in Denver, Colorado.

I've not been able to trace the son he and Maria Yrinea had by the name of Ramon. He is last listed in the Census of 1860, and I don't see him after that.

Jose Julian Espinosa

JOSE JULIAN WAS BORN AT EL RITO, New Mexico on January 4, 1829, the son of Jose Antonio Espinosa and Maria Gertrudis Archuleta. His youth was spent with his parents, and he received his education at the best schools to be found in this country and was also schooled by Father Jose Montano from Spain. He was a very resourceful young man and engaged in the mercantile business at El Rito and successfully engaged the same until 1859, when he sold out. He joined the Army - see below. After his discharge he disposed of his remaining property and moved to Rancho de Taos where he purchased land and engaged in farming and raising stock. He was also involved in the distillery business.

Figure 71 Captain Jose Julian Espinosa - Garcia Collection

Captain Espinosa joined the Union Army on 4 July 1861 at Fort Union, New Mexico where he was commissioned Captain of Company D, 1st Regiment, New Mexico Infantry. He was responsible for raising Company 'D' made up of volunteers at El Rito, New Mexico. The cost of meals for his men was $368.65, transportation was $350 and the rental of rooms for his recruits was $53.42. The value of his horse was $100, and the value of his horse equipment was $41. Understand that this money was all raised by the captain. All the money he spent was never reimbursed to him. His company served as mounted infantry from November 4, 1861 to February 7, 1862 and then as infantry. Part of the reason for going to infantry was that his horses were taken away for use by the Union Army. In February of 1862, his company was engaged as infantry in the Battle of Canoncito (Pigeon's Ranch)

Figure 72 Plaque at Fort Union, NM
- Garcia Collection

Figure 73 Rufina
- Garcia Collection

north of Santa Fe, NM. From March - April of 1862 he fought at the Battle of Valverde where one of his privates, Marcellno Baca was killed. The 1st Infantry New Mexico Volunteers were as follows: Colonel - Kit Carson, Lt Colonel - Francisco Chaves, Major - Arthur Morrison, Company D - Captain Jose Julian Espinosa, 1st Lieutenant - Enriques P Martin, 2nd Lieutenant - Donaciano Montoya, 1st Sergeant - Julian Allures, Sergeant - Jose Maria Chaves, Sergeant - Donación Espinosa, Corporals - Juan Pablo Apodaca, Jose Gabriel Atnecio, Basilio Gallegos, Jose Angel Gallegos, Juan Manuel Gallegos. Captain Jose Julian Espinosa was honorably discharged on May 31, 1862. On March 11,1865 he was still trying to collect the money he spent for raising the company.

After being discharged he went back to El Rito and lived there until 1866 when he moved to Taos, NM. He purchased a large track of land with his brother Juan Antonio and got involved in the cattle business. He then started a flour mill and a distillery. In 1870 Julian with his family moved Southern Colorado, north of Del Norte near Saguache and to a place called El Carnero Creek where he continued in the cattle and sheep business. He served in several county offices, as Road Supervisor, Deputy Assessor, Justice of the Peace and two terms as County Commissioner.

He was a Republican and in their early days was a prominent figure in many of the county and state conventions. He was also sub-agent for the United States Indian Agency, with the Navajos.

While living in Carnero, he was a close friend of the Ute Chief Ouray and his wife Chepita. They were regular guests at his home. He was also friendly with Juan Bautista Pitaval, later Archbishop of Santa Fe, who while at Carnero, baptized Jose Julian's granddaughter, Maria Nicolasa de la Luz (Marie); she was the daughter of his eldest son Celso. He donated ten acres of land and helped build the Carnero Catholic Church. He died in Del Norte on July 12, 1912 at the home of his daughter, Louisa Espinosa de Tafoya, she was formerly the widow of Octaviano Facchinetti, a native of Italy. My brother Cas is standing next to the monument that marks his burial place at the cemetery in Carnero, Colorado (Figure 76).

Figure 74 Jose Julian Espinosa - Garcia Collection

From notes that I have he was a patient man and loved to read, always wore a tie and carried a cane so he could tap his grandson, Amarante to keep him quiet. In his later years after his wife Rufina Montoya passed away, he would spend his summers in Conejos with his daughter Teodora.

According to the notes I found Jose Julian and Rufina Montoya were married February 17, 1852 in Abiquiu, NM. She was the daughter of Marcos Montoya and Maria Ygnacia Mauricia Martinez. I read that they had sixteen children. I've only been able to account for fourteen including Justo, the Native American that they raised. They were as follows; Maria Abelina De Jesus, Jose Celso, Justo, Emerito, Nemesio, Sofia, Carlos, Adelaida, Elisa, Luisa, Ignacia, Teodora, Julian and Leonardo.

Figure 75 Older Julian Espinosa - Garcia Collection

Figure 76 Jose Julian Espinosa Headstone - Garcia Collection

Donaciano Espinosa

DONACIANO WAS THE OLDER BROTHER TO JULIAN, and he was born on May 10, 1826 in El Rito, New Mexico. He was married to Maria Rosa Trujillo and together they had seven children Maria Alcaria, Damian, Dolores, Jose G., Juan Nepomecino, Rosenda and Emiliana. Along with his brother Julian, they settled in the northern end of the San Luis Valley to an area called Carnero. He fought at Valverde and Glorietta Pass during the Civil War and my understanding is that he injured his arm during one of the battles.

Below photos are of Donaciano with his wife Rosa and his final resting place near his brother at the cemetery in Carnero. Photos courtesy of Melissa Espinoza Smart.

Figure 77

Figure 78

Leonardo De Jesus Espinosa

LEONARDO DE JESUS ESPINOSA was Teodora's youngest brother. He was born February 15, 1884, in Carnero, Colorado and baptized February 20, 1884, at Holy Name of Mary Church, Del Norte, Colorado; son of Jose Julian Espinosa and Rufina Montoya. Godparents: Celso Espinosa and Rafaela Martinez, his brother- and sister-in-law.

Figure 79 Leonardo Espinosa – Courtesy Amber Nichols

Leonardo married Fidela Chavez, daughter of Juan Andres Chavez and Candelaria Sanchez, on April 26th, 1904, in Del Norte, Colorado. Together they had six children, Rufinita, Carlos Gilberto, Teresa Pacifica, Adelina Anna, Tobias Julian, and Maria Lucia.

Figure 80 Teresa Pacifica Wedding - Courtesy Amber Nichols

The above photo is Leonardo's daughter, Teresa Pacifica's and her husband Abel Valdez wedding that took place on November 22,1937 in Del Norte, CO. The gentleman behind the groom is my dad, Castelar Garcia. Her brother, Gilbert in top row on the left.

Aurelio Macedonio Espinosa

WE HAD A PICTURE OF THIS GENTLEMAN at the house, and I always wondered who he was. Finally, we were able to make the connection and realized that it was our dad's first cousin, Aurelio Espinosa.

Figure 81 Aurelio Espinosa - Garcia Collection

AURELIO MACEDONIO ESPINOSA.

Born September 12, 1880, at Carnero, Colo. Received his early education in the common schools of Los Mogotes, Colo., and in Grand Junction. Graduated by the Del Norte High School in 1898. In 1901 Mr. Espinosa won the Giffin Prize Debate. 1901-02, Assistant in Romance Languages, U. of C.; 1902, Instructor in Modern Languages, University of New Mexico; in 1904, Professor of Modern Languages, and in 1906, Professor of Romance Langnages in the same university. Received the degree Ph. B. in 1902 and M. A. in 1904, both at the U. of C. His M. A. thesis was an annotated edition of Jose Echegaray's "El Grau Galeote," which is now used at the following universities: California, Colorado, Kansas, Ohio, Texas, Columbia, Harvard, John Hopkins, Colorado College, New Mexico and other schools. He has recently published another edition of one of Echegaray's plays, which bids fair to rival the other in popularity. He is working now to receive the degree Ph. D. from the University of Chicago, his subject being, "New Mexican Spanish Dialect." During the summers of 1904 and 1905 he was instructor in Spanish and French at the U. of C. Summer School and at the Colorado-Texas Chautauqua. The coming summer Mr. Espinosa will be holding classes at the University of Chicago.

Figure 82 Aurelio Espinosa - Garcia Collecton

Aurelio's father was Jose Celso Espinosa born on March 28, 1856 in El Rito, New Mexico. He married Rafelita Antonia Martinez on January 14, 1878 in Carnero, Colorado. They had fourteen children, Tobias, Aurelio, Jose Celso, Maria Nicolaza, the first Imelda, died of scarlet fever, the second Imelda married Dennis Chavez, first Hispanic from New Mexico, to be elected into the Unites States Senate, Maria Del Carmen, Jose Ramon, Rosalina, Antonio Gilberto, Jose Edmundo, Josefa Rufina, Ernesto and Luis Guillermo. Celso and Rafelita's children were able to attend college and have very successful careers.

Garcia Family

THIS NEXT SECTION WILL FEATURE some of our relatives from the Garcia family that have since passed but left a legacy behind. We will be discussing both of our grandfather's families. From his first wife, Sofia we have Alejandro, Candelaria, Reginaldo, Placida and Rufina. Irinea and Julianita passed away at an early age. Irinea was thirteen and Juliana was just seven when they passed. From his second wife, Teodora's family we have Sofia, Victor, Nea, Amarante, Julian, Avelina, Castelar and Sevilla.

Grandfather Jose Amarante believed in education and all of his children graduated from high school and all of them except for Castelar and Sevilla were able to advance their education and graduate from a college or university.

In a time when not too many girls went to college, he made sure his daughters received a good education. They all went out and made a huge difference in the world. I am sure if he was alive, he would have been immensely proud of his girls.

Alejandro Garcia

ALEJANDRO WAS OUR GRANDFATHER, Jose Amarante Garcia's first-born son. He attended Barnes Commercial College in Denver in 1904 and graduated with honours. He returned home at the age of twenty to assist his father with the cattle and sheep and at the age of twenty-one drowned in the Chama River, near Chama, New Mexico in May of 1905. The story is that he had discovered gold in Cumbres the year before but never told anyone where he found it.

Figure 83 Alejandro Garcia - Garcia Collection

Maria Candelaria Garcia Chacon

CANDELARIA WAS THE FIRST BORN of the Jose Amarante Garcia family. She was born on April 11, 1882 in Conejos, CO. She married Louis Onesimo Chacon on June 29, 1904. The story is that when she married, her father gave her and her husband a thousand dollars as a wedding gift, quite a sum of money back in 1904.

Onesimo came from a very distinguished family in the valley and one of the things he enjoyed doing was playing baseball for the local town team. Seems that he was a pretty good ball player.

Candelaria and Onesimo had ten children. Unfortunately some passed away at birth or at a young age.

Candelaria was just a month shy of being 102 when she passed away.

Candelaria received a letter from President Ronald Reagan dated April 16, 1982 congratulating her on celebrating her 100th Birthday.

Louis Onesimo Chacon

L.O. Chacon's family arrived in the Conejos area in about 1855. His father Juan Francisco Chacon was elected senator from Distric 19 to the first Colorado State Legislature. L.O. married the oldest daughter of Jose Amarante Garcia... Candelaria Garcia. Together they were very active in the political debates in early 1900's. Candelaria marched and took part in the women's sufferage, which gave her and all women the right to vote. L. O. served as Conejos's game warden and many other local government positions.

Figure 84 Courtesy Gerri Chacon

Easter Sunday Marks 100th Birthday

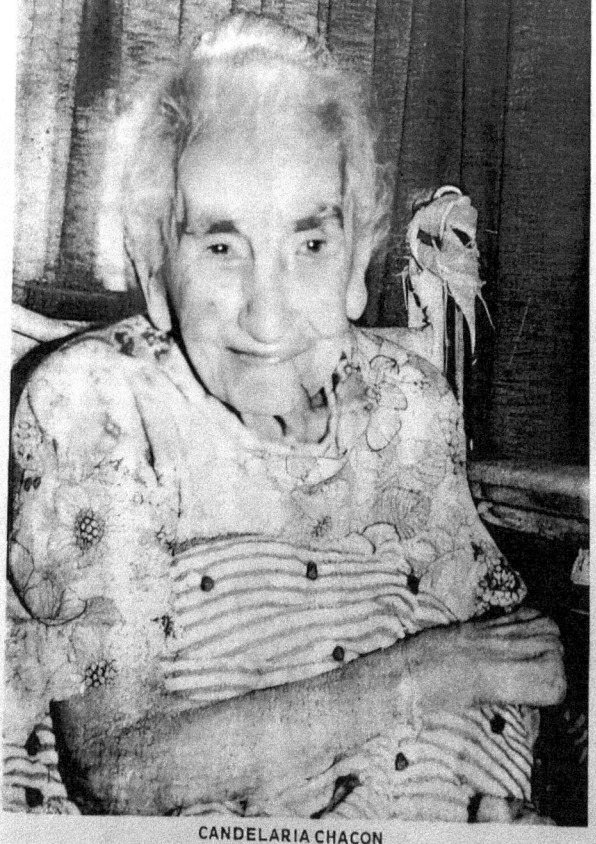

CANDELARIA CHACON

By LYNNE HEADLEE
Courier Correspondent

Mrs. Candelaria G. Chacon will celebrate her 100th birthday at Evergreen Nursing Home on Easter Sunday.

An open house, 2-4 p.m. will be held in her honor by her only surviving child and his wife, Mr. and Mrs. Ray Chacon, of Antonito, and her grandchildren. All friends and relatives are invited to attend.

Mrs. Chacon is a descendent of an aristocratic family. Her grandfather, Jose Victor Garcia, served in the New Mexico State Legislature and the Territorial Legislature in the 1850s.

Her father, J. Amarante Garcia, was a Colorado State Representative for the area now including Conejos and Costilla counties before the two were divided. He was also Conejos County sheriff for many years.

Mrs. Chacon was born in Los Brazos, a settlement east of Antonito. She was the oldest of 19 children.

She married a rancher and farmer, Louis O. Chacon, in 1904. They attended the World Fair in St. Louis on their honeymoon, returning to live on a ranch west of Antonito. Although the couple helped raise her brothers and sisters after her mother's death, they had 10 children of their own.

"Mother said that one of the saddest days of her life was when her oldest boy fell down a well when he was 12 years old, landed on an upright bolt and was killed," said Ray's wife, Cora.

"She was of true pioneer stock," she continued. "She raised her own turkeys and chickens, and always had a big

Figure 85 Candelaria's 100th - Gerri Chacon

For Antonito's Candelaria Chacon

garden, which she tended, and she had the most wonderful big family dinners!"

Although considered wealthy in the standards of time, Candelaria Chacon worked hard caring for her family. She was well educated, having received her schooling at Mount St. Scholastica Academy in Canon City, under the sisters of the Order of St. Benedict, and the sisters of Loretto in Conejos and the Loretto Academy in Pueblo.

She taught school for many years after receiving her teaching certificate. She was an avid reader until her eyesight started to fail.

"Her handwriting has always

been beautiful," Ray exclaimed.

She was also a telephone exchange operator in Conejos for many years.

Her husband, Louis, a graduate of Sacred Heart College of Denver, now Regis College, was a member of the original school board in Conejos and was Conejos County clerk. He also served as game warden for many years, retiring 20 days

before his death in 1936.

In her later years she lived in a house in Antonito built by Ray.

"It (her home) was always open to all the grandkids and she became 'grandma' to most of the kids in town. They always stopped by her place to visit and have some of the delicious treats she prepared," said Cora.

Mrs. Chacon has been a

resident of Evergreen Nursing Home since 1975.

She has 104 grandchildren, including 66 great grandchildren and 23 great-great grandchildren.

Five of her sisters, Sister William Joseph, Loretto Academy, El Paso, Texas; Mrs. Reginaldo Garcia, Mrs. Avelina Vigil, and Mrs. Castelar Garcia, Antonito; and Mrs. Maclovio Gallegos Garciaj San Luis, plan to celebrate her birthday with her.

Mrs. Chacon attributes her long life to hard work and an intense thirst for knowledge and love of fellow man.

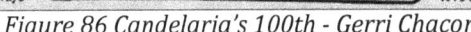

Figure 86 Candelaria's 100th - Gerri Chacon

Figure 87 Candelaria & Louis – Gerri Chacon

The ten children they had together were: Josephine Marie (Josefa), Maria Sofia, Elena, Louis Onesimo, Rufina Thelma, Alejandro, Jeffre, Alejandro Francisco, Maria Candelaria Margareta, Amarante Alejandro and Ramon Alfonzo.

Their two sons Alejandro and Ramon would serve in the military during World War II.

Figure 88 is of Louis with his father Juan Francisco Chacon. My understanding is that the Chacon family were very wealthy with ranches and livestock.

Figure 88 Louise & Juan Francisco - Gerri Chacon

Figure 89 Sofia Chacon - Garcia Collection

This photo of Sofia Chacon in front of the mirror with her reflection is a classic. Unfortunately she would pass away at the age of twenty-nine.

Figure 90 Chacon Children - Gerri Chacon

The above photo shows the Chacon children – back row; Thelma, Alejandro, Josephine Marie and bottom row; Rufina, Ramon and Elena.

Figure 91 Candelaria & children - Gerri Chacon

The above photo shows Candelaria with her children. From left to right: Helen, Ramon, Candelaria, Alejandro, and Josephine.

Reginaldo Garcia

REGINALDO GARCÍA WAS BORN on April 2, 1888, in El Carnero, Saguache County, Colorado. Much like his older brother Alejandro, he would pursue his education at Barnes Business College on the Regis campus. Upon completing his studies, he returned to Conejos and was involved with his father's ranching business and eventually acquired his own ranch where he raised both cattle and sheep.

Reginaldo held a number of public offices and much like his father he was Conejos County Sheriff and County Judge.

Figure 92 Reginaldo - Garcia Collection

Reginaldo Garcia

Born 1888, Carnero, Saguache County, Colorado
Dates served in Colorado Legislature:
1927-1929 House

Reginaldo Garcia represented the third generation from his family to serve in the Colorado General Assembly. His grandfather, Jose Victor Garcia, came to Colorado in 1853 and served nine years in the Territorial House and Territorial Council during the 1860's and early 1870's. His father, Jose A. Garcia, held the post of Conejos County sheriff for nineteen years and also served as a Republican in the House from 1881-1883. Thus, Reginaldo Garcia traced his roots to some of Colorado's earliest pioneers and belonged to a family held in high esteem throughout the region.

He was educated in the public schools of Conejos and subsequently pursued a course of study at Barnes Business College on the Regis University campus. Upon completing his studies, he returned to Conejos County, where he pursued the raising of both sheep and cattle along the Conejos River. He served several terms as Secretary of the Conejos County Sheep Growers Association and served as Vice President of the Commercial State Bank of Antonito.

Mr. Garcia held a variety of public offices during his lifetime, including Conejos County Sheriff, Conejos County Judge, and County Treasurer, in which capacity he was reelected for several terms. Volume five of the *History of Colorado*, published in 1927, noted that he had made "a splendid record in that capacity."

In 1926 he was elected as a Republican to serve in the House, representing Conejos County. In the twenty-sixth session of the Colorado General Assembly he was responsible for carrying House Bill No. 58—"an act relating to the drainage of the state lands and providing an appropriation to carry out the provisions hereof"

(House Journal of the General Assembly of the State of Colorado: Twenty-Sixth Session, page 1131). He also forwarded legislation for the maintenance of Pike Memorial Park and for the regulation of fish and game.

Figure 93 Reginaldo - Gerri Chacon

Figure 94 Reginaldo & Rosa - Carmel Cortez Garrett

Reginaldo and Rosa on their wedding day (Figure 94). They had five children, Reginaldo II, Crestino, Rosa and two infant daughters who died at birth. Both of their sons served in the military during World War II.

Figure 95 shows Reginaldo with his wife Rosita, Teodora, his father, Jose Amarante. The little girl behind them is Avelina and the baby on his mother's lap is our dad, Castelar.

Their son Reginaldo II (Figure 97) served in the US Army during World War II and followed in his father's footsteps by serving as Conejos County Clerk and ranching. He married Otilda Olguin from San Luis and had three children, Reginaldo III, Carlos & Roberto.

Figure 95 Reginaldo with Jose Amarante - Carmel Cortez Garrett

*Figure 96 Reginaldo & Rosa 50th
- Gerri Chacon*

*Figure 97 Reginaldo II
– Reggie Garcia*

Figure 98 Reggie & Otilda - Garcia Collection

Above photo is Reggie and his wife Otilda in front of their home in Antonito.

My mom used to visit Tia Rosita, as we knew her, at her home in Antonito. Her son Crestino used to keep the yard looking like a garden from *Better Homes and Gardens*. Rosa lived to the ripe old age of one hundred and four (Figure 99).

ALBINA ROSA GARCIA
Antonito homemaker, 104

ANTONITO — Albina Rosa Garcia, 104, died July 3, 2001, at the Conejos County Hospital in La Jara.

She was born March 8, 1897, in Los Fuertecitos to Jose and Piedad Pena Romero, and was united in marriage to Reginaldo Garcia Sr. on Jan. 15, 1914.

A homemaker, she was a member of the Sagrado Corazon and Las Fatimas De Antonito. Her hobbies included fishing, crocheting, quilting, gardening and especially the time she spent with her loving family.

Survivors include three grandsons, Reginaldo O. Garcia (Betty Goulden) of Monte Vista, Carlos (Ramona) Garcia of Antonito, and Roberto Garcia of Antonito; seven great-grandchildren; and several nieces, nephews and cousins.

Rosa was preceded in death by her parents, her husband and all of her children, including two infant daughters; a daughter, Rosa, two sons, Reginaldo Garcia Jr. and Crestino Garcia; and all of her brothers and sisters.

A Vigil Service with Recitation of the Rosary will be held at 7 p.m. Thursday, July 5, at the Romero Chapel in Antonito.

Another Rosary will be held at 7 p.m. Friday, July 6, at the Saint Augustine Church in Antonito.

Funeral Services will be held at 10 a.m. Saturday, July 7, at Our Lady of Guadalupe Church in Conejos, with burial following in the La Jara Cemetery.

Friends may call from 1 to 8 p.m. Thursday and Friday at the Romero Chapel in Antonito who is in care of the arrangements.

Figure 99 Rosa's Obit - Gerri Chacon

91

Placida Garcia Smith

PLACIDA ELVIRA GARCIA SMITH was described as a patriot, a woman who lived her life teaching, sharing, and caring for others. Born August 7, 1896, in Conejos, Colorado, she began her teaching career shortly after graduating from Loretto Academy in Pueblo, Colorado. From then until 1928 she taught, rising to the position of principal at

Figure 100 Placida Garcia Smith - Garcia Collection

Conejos Grade School and later becoming Deputy County Ttreasurer of Conejos County.

Meanwhile, she continued her education, studying summers at Greeley State Teachers College and the University of Mexico in Mexico City before receiving her bachelor's degree in 1927 from the University of Utah with a major in Spanish and a minor in Sociology. She did graduate work at the University of California in Berkeley and also at the University of Denver.

In 1928, Placida Smith moved to Phoenix when her husband, Reginald G. Smith, took a job at what is now Phoenix Newspapers Inc. She became involved with the community, first working as a substitute teacher in Phoenix Elementary School and Phoenix Union High Schools.

Her major civic contribution began in 1931 when she assumed the directorship of Friendly House, a center for immigrants trying to learn the ways of their adopted country. At Friendly House, men found help in getting jobs; women learned American housekeeping skills, and some found domestic service jobs.

All learned English and what it meant to be American citizens. Placida strived to impress those in her classes that they were special. "You came to this country because you wanted to, and now you want to become citizens," she would say. Under her tutelage, 1,400 people became United States' citizens. "In helping them attain their goal she instilled in them an understanding that freedom to an American is more than merely a word.

It is a spirit and a way of life," said U.S. District County Judge Valdemar A. Cordova in a letter nominating Placida Garcia Smith for the Arizona Women's Hall of Fame. For her efforts, in 1953 she was presented with the Daughters of the American Revolution award of merit. In 1962, she was chosen Phoenix Woman of the Year by the Phoenix Advertising Club. In 1982 she was elected to the Arizona's Women's Hall of Fame. She was active in commercial real estate and made quite a name for herself.

Placida married Reginald G Smith on June 9, 1928 in San Francisco, California. Together they had a son also named Reginald.

Reginald Smith II was born March 25, 1930 in Phoenix, Arizona and married Margorie Felder Johnson on April 1, 1940 and they had three children; Douglas, Sharon and Leslie. Reginald passed away on April 15, 2008 in Phoenix, Arizona. Margorie passed away on April 28, 2012 in Sebring, Highlands County, Florda.

Placida Garcia Smith dies; church, community leader

Placida Garcia Smith, 84, who had been a church and community leader and director of Friendly House for more than 30 years, died July 15, 1981, in the Village Green Nursing Home.

Mrs. Smith came to the Valley in 1928 with her husband, Reginald G. Smith, a former reporter for what is now Phoenix Newspapers Inc.

In 1931, she was appointed director of Friendly House, which offered a social program and related services for the foreign-born. It is now a United Way agency.

She taught citizenship, and under her direction, about 1,400 people became citizens.

Among other activities, Mrs. Smith was a Spanish instructor for the American Institute of Foreign Trade. In 1946, she went to Mexico as the official representative of that group.

She also was a social worker at a Japanese reloca- tion center near Chandler. She was a member of St. Mary's Altar Society, Vista, Altrusa and Pan American clubs.

The Phoenix Advertising Club selected Mrs. Smith as Phoenix Woman of the Year in 1961 for her outstanding contributions to the community. She received numerous awards, including the Award of Merit from the Daughters of the American Revolution and the University of Arizona's 75th Anniversary Award.

She was born in Conejos, Colo., where her family settled in the early 1850s. She was a graduate of the University of Utah and attended the University of Mexico in Mexico City and the University of California at Berkeley.

Survivors include her son, Reginald G.; three grandchildren; a brother; and four sisters.

Mass will be at noon Thursday in St. Thomas the Apostle Catholic Church, 24th Street and Campbell. Friends may call after 4 p.m. Wednesday in Whitney & Murphy Arcadia Funeral Home, 4800 E. Indian School.

Figure 101 Placida Garcia Smith - Gerri Chacon

Sister William Joseph

EARLY ON IN HER LIFE RUFINA felt a call in her heart to become a Nun and follow that vocation. As a sign of her new life, she chose the name of Sister William Joseph.

Figure 102 Sister William Joseph - Garcia Collection

Sister William Joseph attended and graduated from the Sisters of Loretto Academy in Denver. She graduated from the University of Denver with a Bachelor's Degree. She did graduate work at Creighton University in Nebraska and obtained her Master's Degree in language from the University of Denver. She taught for 57 years in Denver, St. Louis, and El Paso. She retired to Nazareth Hall a retirement home for the Sisters of Loretto in El Paso, Texas. She enjoyed reading the newspaper every day and magazines. She especially enjoyed reading biographies. Sister William Joseph would also visit the hospital and especially the older folks that were in the psychiatric ward.

Figure 103 Sister William Joseph - Gerri Chacon

Sofia Garcia Cortez

SOFIA WAS THE FIRST BORN of Jose Amarante's second family with his wife Teodora.

Figure 104 Cortez Wedding - Carmel Cortez Garrett

She was born on January 10, 1900 in Conejos and attended and graduated from Loretto Academy in Pueblo. She would meet Ezekiel C. Cortez and they would marry August 4, 1920 in Conejos, Colorado. Together they had three boys, Ezekiel, Hernan and Hubert. After eleven years of marriage, Sofia was divorced from her husband and as a single mother she raised her three sons.

She taught school and worked with Social Services in Santa Fe, New Mexico eventually working her way up to Director.

Sofia's first son was Ezekiel born on April 30, 1921 in Antonito, Colorado. He attended elementary school in La Isla where his mother taught in a one room school house and eventually moved to Santa Fe,

Figure 105 Hernan, Hubert, Sofia & Ezekiel - Carmel Cortez Garrett

Figure 106 Ezekiel Cortez - Carmel Cortez Garrett

New Mexico where he graduated from Santa Fe High School. He then attended and graduated from New Mexico A & M College. He attended George Washington University Law School gaining a Bachelor's Degree in Literature. In 1942, he graduated from the University of Norte Dame in Indiana and received his commission as an Ensign in the United States Navy Reserve on September 22, 1943.

During World War II, Ezekiel participated in the invasion of France and Anzio Beachhead in Italy. He was active during the Korean Conflict. According to his autobiography – *The Life and Times of Commander E. C. Cortez* in 1942, he was engaged in building detention camps in Roswell, New Mexico and Douglas, Arizona for the Japanese Americans living in the United States by order of President Roosevelt.

Ezekiel married Francis Sanchez from Santa Fe, New Mexico and together they had three children, Louis Renee, Carla and Carmel. Louis, and Carmel would follow their father and join the US Navy. Carmel retired after an exciting career seeing the world and make her home in New Mexico to be near her parents.

Figure 107 Hernan Cortez – Eric Cortez

Hernan was the second son, and he was born on April 22, 1922. He went to the University of Southern California and graduated with a Civil Engineering degree. During World War II he served as an Engineering Officer during the invasion of Guam in July of 1944. He was working for the Bechtel Corp in Mexico City when he passed away. He was married to Adeline Gutierrez and they had three children Eric, Duke and Christina.

Hubert was the youngest son and he was born on September 7, 1923 in Pueblo, Colorado. He would enter the Army Air Corp as a pilot and was with the American Air Force in Italy during World War II. He unfortunately died in an airplane crash while training a young pilot in Texas on January 8, 1948. He was married to Fredda Mae Gonzales and had one son, Carl Theodore.

Figure 108 Hubert Cortez - Carmel Cortez Garrett

Victor Garcia

VICTOR WAS BORN ON NOVEMBER 29, 1901 in Conejos, Colorado. Like his siblings he would get a very good education.

Figure 109 Victor Garcia - Theresa Topoleski

He was not quite seventeen when his father passed away. Along with his older brother, Reginaldo, he was responsible for taking care of the ranch and animals. He was elected to Conejos County Assessor and eventually worked for the Colorado Department of Personnel. Victor and Candelaria Lucero met and married in Conejos, Colorado on November 26, 1925. Together they had two children, Victor Jr. and Consuelo.

Figure 110 Victor & Candelaria Wedding - Theresa Topoleski

*Figure 111 Victor & Pat
- Theresa Topoleski*

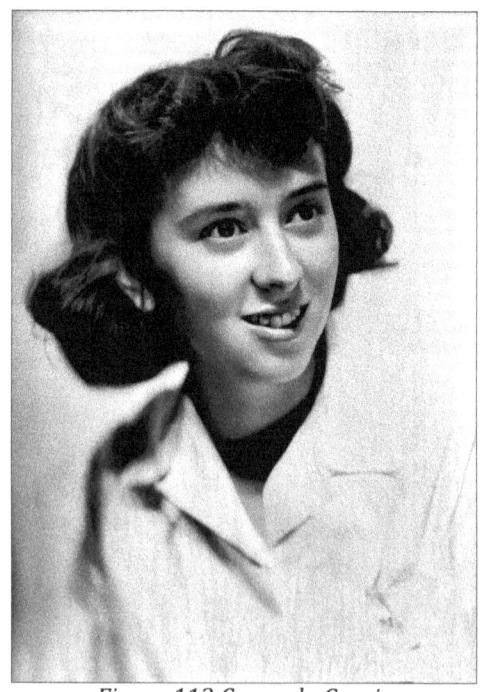

*Figure 112 Consuelo Garcia
– Garcia Collection*

Nea Garcia Gallegos

NEA WAS BORN ON AUGUST 1, 1903 in Conejos, Colorado to Teodora and Jose Amarante Garcia. She attended school in Conejos and later enrolled at the Loretto Academy for Girls in Pueblo. She graduated from Antonito High School in 1922.

She earned a Teaching Certificate and taught school in Antonito where she had the opportunity to teach her brother and our dad, Castelar. Always eager to learn she attended Adams State College in Alamosa, Western State College in Gunnison and the University of Utah in Salt Lake City where her older sister Placida was

Figure 113 Nea Garcia - Francisco Gallegos

teaching. In 1934, she was appointed Postmaster of the Post Office in San Luis and would serve in that capacity until her retirement at age of seventy-one. Her daughter Pepita took over as Postmaster.

She married Maclovio Gallegos on January 15, 1933 in Alamosa, and the marriage report records the county as Costilla, Colorado.

Together they had seven children all of whom would graduate from college. Their children were Pepita, Francisco, Loyola, Teodora, Marcella, Ozella and Maclovio. Nea was inducted into the Colorado Women's Hall of Fame in 2012 for her involvement in the field of education.

NEA G. GALLEGOS
Former San Luis postmistress, 99

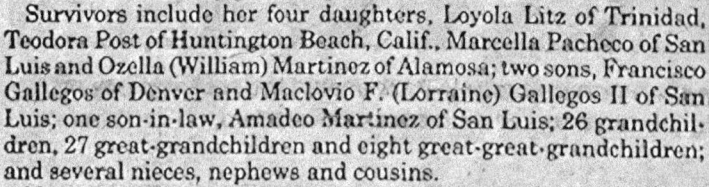

SAN LUIS — Nea G. Gallegos, 99, died Aug. 28, 2002 at the San Luis Care Center in Alamosa.

She was born Aug. 1, 1903 in Conejos to Jose Amarante and Teodora Espinoza Garcia. Her father, Jose Amarante Garcia, was well known as a county sheriff and county judge of Conejos County.

Nea was a primary school teacher and Postmistress in San Luis for 43 years, and a member of the National and San Luis Valley Post Masters Association.

Her hobbies included crocheting, tatting, embroidering, stamp collecting, reading, writing, gardening and traveling. She treasured family gatherings and celebrations.

Survivors include her four daughters, Loyola Litz of Trinidad, Teodora Post of Huntington Beach, Calif., Marcella Pacheco of San Luis and Ozella (William) Martinez of Alamosa; two sons, Francisco Gallegos of Denver and Maclovio F. (Lorraine) Gallegos II of San Luis; one son-in-law, Amadeo Martinez of San Luis; 26 grandchildren, 27 great-grandchildren and eight great-great-grandchildren; and several nieces, nephews and cousins.

Nea was preceded in death by her husband, Maclovio Gallegos; one daughter, Pepita Martinez, one granddaughter, Anita Litz; three great-grandchildren, Peita Martinez, Tomas Mondragon and Luis Sandoval, as well as all her brothers and sisters.

A Vigil Service with Recitation of the Rosary will be at 7 p.m. Friday, Aug. 30, at Sangre de Cristo Catholic Church in San Luis.

Funeral Services will be at 1 p.m. Saturday, Aug. 31, at the same church, with burial following in the Sangre de Cristo Cemetery at San Luis.

Contributions may be made to the Sangre De Cristo Parish, P.O. Box 326 in San Luis, CO 81152.

Family and friends may call from 10 a.m. to 5 p.m. Friday and from 10 a.m. to noon Saturday at the Romero Funeral Chapel in San Luis, which is handling the arrangements.

Figure 114 Obiturary Nea Gallegos - Gerri Chacon

The photo below (Figure 116) shows Nea top left and her sister, Placida on the bottom right when they were attending college in Utah together.

Interesting story about my Tia as I remember it. In the mid-seventies, she had flown to California to see her daughter Teddy. She wanted to bring back her youngest granddaughter and namesake Nea with her to Colorado. She made it to the airport and mistakenly caught a flight going to Hawaii. I am told that the airline treated her and the granddaughter very well. They put

Figure 115 Nea & Maclovio - Francisco Gallegos

her up in a nice hotel and put them on a flight home the next day. I believe they even got leis. What a wonderful experience!

Figure 116 Nea and her sister Placida - Carmel Cortez Garrett

Figure 117 Nea & Maclovio with grandchildren
- Francisco Gallegos

When I had the opportunity to visit my Tia she loved to talk about her father, mother, and her family. You could tell she was immensely proud of them. Before she passed, I went to see her at the nursing home and I introduced myself as Michael, "El hijo de Castelar." She came back and said, "Te vas a casar?" Then she realized who I was.

Figure 118 is Nea's family, starting with Marcella, Maclovio, Teodora, Francisco, Loyola and Ozella.

Figure 118 Gallegos Family - Francisco Gallegos

Unfortunately for Tia Nea, her oldest daughter Pepita passed away February of 1986 along with her great grandson, Tomas. Pepita was the Postmaster of the Post Office in San Luis, Colorado at the time of her passing. The few times I did get to see her she was so full of life and laughter, and it was a treat to be around her.

Figure 119 Nea, Pepita & Francisco
- Francisco Gallegos

Jose Amarante Garcia Jr.

JOSE AMARANTE WAS BORN ON SEPTEMBER 6, 1905 in Conejos, Colorado. He attended and graduated from Antonito High School. Following high school, he attended Sacred Heart College and returned home to help with the ranch. He eventually went into the ranching business himself. Amarante met and married Margaret Sargent on March 17, 1935 in Antonito, CO. Together they had three children, Maria Teresa who passed away in 1961, Jose Amarante Eduardo who passed away in 2010, and Reyes who received his Doctorate in Philosophy from the University of Colorado. Jose Amarante would eventually move to San Diego and work for the Department of Defense.

Figure 120 Margaret & Amarante - Reyes Garcia

The photo (Figure 121) is of Tio Amarante, Tia Sevilla and Julian discussing their father Jose Amarante Garcia and it was featured in the June 6, 1958 San Diego newspaper. The book Amarante is holding was a history of people who were instrumental in helping to develop the state of Colorado and our ancestors are in it. The album that Sevilla is

Figure 121 Amarante, Sevilla & Julian - Garcia Collection

holding is a photo album of the Garcia family. The pistol that Julian is holding belonged to our grandfather, Jose Amarante Garcia who used it when he was the Sheriff of Conejos County.

Margaret was from the Sargent and Gonzales families who had extensive land holdings that were one time part of the Tierra Amarilla Land Grant in New Mexico and Colorado.

I was about eight years old when they told me that my cousin Teresa had passed away. I always wanted to know what she looked like and fortunately her daughter Vicki Graham had a couple of photos. (Figures 122 & 123)

Tia Margaret was born on November 12, 1905 in Rio Arriba, New Mexico to John Sargent and Lugarda Gonzales. Her sisters were Mercedes Middlemist and Dora Quinlan. After the death of her husband, Tia Margaret moved back to the valley and the ranch. There are a couple of photos of her two sons, Jose and Reyes (Figures 124 & 125) on page 113.

111

A couple pieces of property once owned by my Tio Amarante held some interesting historical significance. The property in Guadalupe is where the first settlement took place. My father would mention to my brother and sister that it was at Servilleta that the settlers first settled in 1854. The property is now owned by the Moellers. The other property was in Cumbres. In 1848 a battle took place between the Ute and Apaches against the Union Army. A famous scout by the name of Bill Williams was injured there. More about this later in the book.

Figure 122 Teresa - Vicki Graham

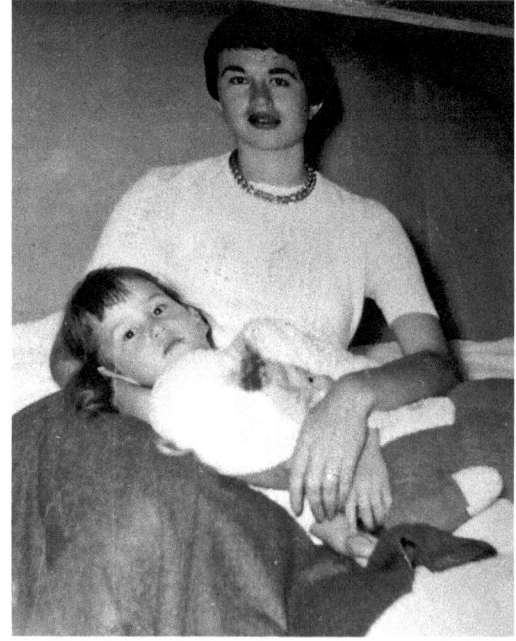

Figure 123 Teresa & Vicki - Vicki Graham

Figure 124 Jose - Reyes Garcia

Figure 125 Reyes - Reyes Garcia

113

Julian Garcia

JULIAN GARCIA WAS BORN ON FEBRUARY 24, 1908 in Conejos, Colorado. Dad used to say that Julian was quite the athlete. His 1927 Antonito High School shows him playing basketball, football and running track. Another interesting bit of information is that he went to Conejos High School for his freshman year, and Antonito High for his Sophomore year. He moved to Regis High School in Denver for his Junior year and came back to Antonito High for his Senior year.

Julian furthered his education and worked on the ranch. He eventually made his way to San Diego, California along with his brother Amarante and his sister Sevilla. He was employed by the California Department of Personnel. He met his and married his wife, Carmela Gaouna. She was known for her ability to make the best tortillas.

Figure 126 Julian - Aglay Garcia

Figure 127 Julian & Castelar - Garcia Collection

Figure 128 Julian - Aglay Garcia

Figure 129 photo shows Julian's son Julian II, his granddaughter Katrina, his daughter Aglay, his wife Carmela, his granddaughter, Teresa and his son, Hector and Peggy Abbott.

Figure 129 Julian Garcia Family - Aglay Garcia

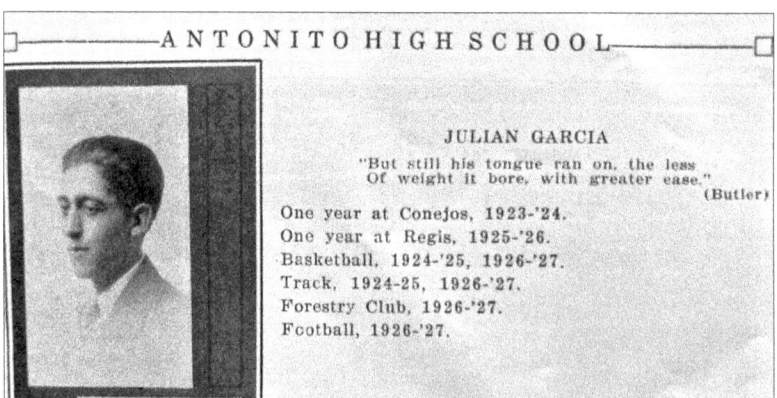

Figure 130 Julian - Aglay Garcia

Avelina Garcia Vigil

AVELINA WAS BORN ON DECEMBER 28, 1909 in Conejos, Colorado. She would attend the Conejos schools and one year of Conejos High School and a half year in Pueblo and then graduated from Antonito High School with her brother, Julian in 1927. After high school she attended college and eventually received her teaching certificate. She taught school in Antonito. She met and married Patrick Vigil on August 20, 1920 and together they had a daughter, Carmen.

Figure 131 Avelina - Garcia Collection

Figure 132 Garcia/Vigil Wedding - Garcia Collection

The key to the above Garcia/Vigil wedding.

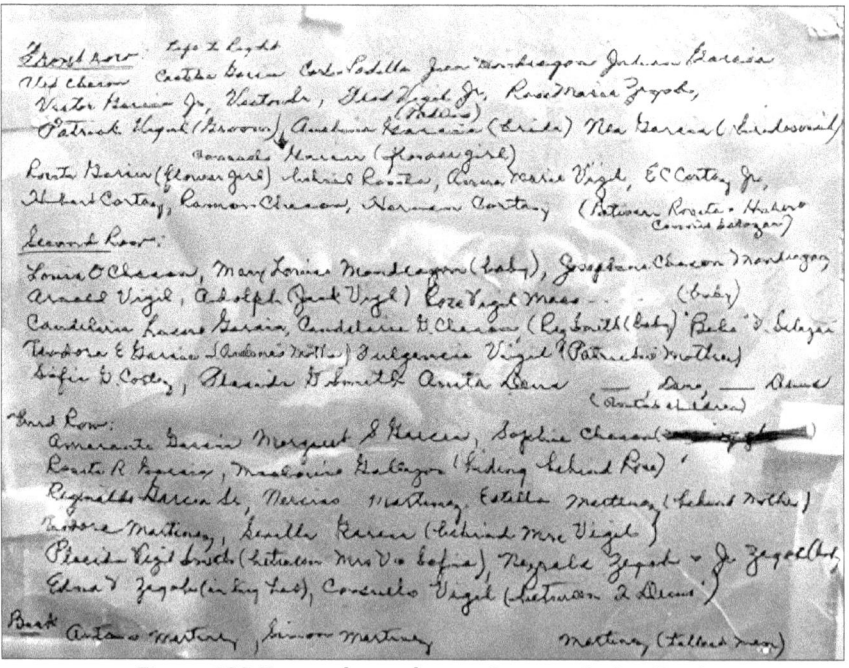

Figure 133 Key to above photo – Carmen Ortiz y Davis

Figure 134 Carmen - Garcia Collection

Figure 135 Avelina & Patrick

The above photo shows Avelina, Teodora, Geraldine, Carmen, Patrick, Charles II, Charles and Sevilla. Courtesy of Aglay Garcia.

Aunt Avelina and Uncle Pat would often come to the house for the holidays. Uncle Pat loved to fly fish, and he loved to go on the Conejos River next to the Broyles bridge in Canon. Tia Avelina had diabetes, but she would monitor it and controlled it by her diet. I was told that she would also help other individuals to control their blood sugar. My aunt passed away on December 16, 1993 at the hospital in La Jara. I remember my uncle Pat said that if she passed away that he would follow her, and sure enough about a week later he passed away on December 23, 1993.

Sevilla Garcia Trambley

SEVILLA WAS BORN ON JUNE 28, 1914 in Conejos, Colorado. She would attend and graduate from Antonito High School in 1932. Sevilla went to nursing school and eventually got her RN degree. She moved to San Diego at an early age. She met and married Charles Trambley who was a Prize Fighter at the time. She told him that he needed to find some other line of work before she would marry him. Together they had two children, Geraldine and Charles Jr. We don't have many photos of her or her family.

Sevilla passed away on February 1, 1975 in San Diego, California and Charles passed away on January 27, 1994.

Figure 138 is of Charles and Geraldine Trambley at a young age.

Figure 136 Sevilla - Garcia Collection

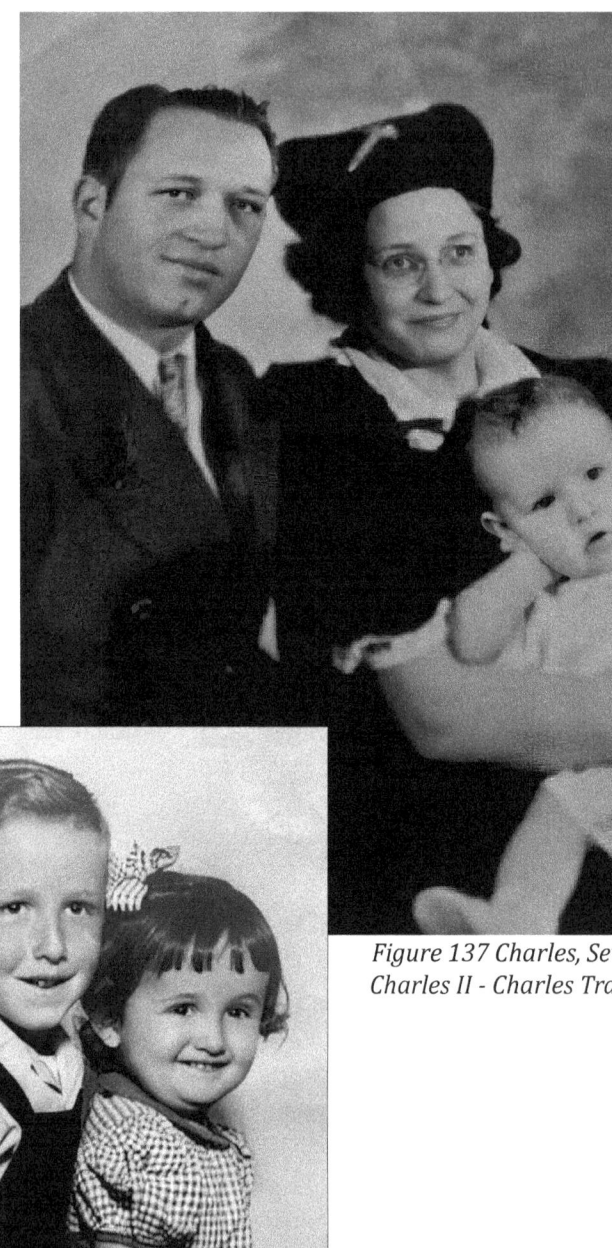

Figure 137 Charles, Sevilla &
Charles II - Charles Trambley

Figure 138 Charles & Geraldine
- Garcia Collection

Our Lady of Guadalupe Church

FATHER SALVADOR PERSONE was the first Jesuit and third priest to serve Our Lady of Guadalupe parish starting in 1871. The Jesuits served from 1871 to 1920, and they were followed by the Theatine Order.

Father Pascal Tomassini had the longest length of service to the parish of the Jesuits, remaining seven years in three different rotations.

He offered the last prayer to Abraham Ortiz on his hanging in 1889. When doing research on the family history I found his name on a lot of baptisms and marriages. Our family worshiped and supported Our Lady of Guadalupe Church and parish from its inception.

A convent had been built next to the church in 1877 by the Jesuits and Sacred Heart Academy was established and the students were taught by the nuns from the Sisters of Loretto.

Figure 139 Father Salvador Persone - Jesuit Beginning in New Mexico

On Ash Wednesday in 1926, Our Lady of Guadalupe church was being heated up for the morning services when it caught on fire, and before it could be contained it was destroyed. Interesting that almost ninety years later, the church caught on fire again but fortunately it was not destroyed.

The following photos on the fire of 1926 came from my cousin Theresa Topoleski.

Figure 140 Father Tomassini
- Garcia Collection

Figure 141 Our Lady of Guadalupe Church

Figure 142 Church Fire - Theresa Topoleski

Figure 143 Church Fire - Theresa Topoleski

Figure 144 1926 Church Fire - Theresa Topoleski

Figure 145 Church Bell - Theresa Topoleski

Figure 146 Teodora helping with clean up - Theresa Topoleski

After the fire, my grandmother helped to organize the women to help the men with the clean-up. The photo on the previous page Figure 146 shows our grandmother serving lunch to the men. She is the lady with the black hat and coat.

I was visiting my cousin Carmen Oriz y Davis in her home in Albuquerque, NM when I happen to see this painting of the church in Conejos. The church was destroyed by fire on Ash Wednesday in 1926 and was rebuilt in 1927. She had an artist by the name G L Bromin do a painting of the new church.

With permission of my cousin, I am sharing this painting.

Figure 147 Painting of church 1927 - Carmen Ortiz y Davis

Flood of 1911

MY FATHER TOLD ME ABOUT this flood and at one time we had pictures, unfortunately they disappeared. This account taken from the *Ledger News*, October 7, 1911. The rain began to come down in torrents on Wednesday, October 4, 1911 and continued for seventy-two hours. Within twelve hours over four inches of rain had been recorded at Cumbres. By Thursday night the Rio Grande, Conejos, San Antonio and other rivers were flooding. In many communities water flooded into the houses causing residents to remove furniture and to shovel mud from their floors. The village of Guadalupe lay under a foot of water and Conejos Canyon was especially ravaged by the waters and large numbers of cattle drowned and were scattered along the river.

Figure 148 1911 Flood – 1911 Ledger News

Cumbres

CUMBRES HAS ALWAYS HAD A SPECIAL PLACE in the hearts of the Garcia Family. Our dad and mom would spend their summers in the place we call Heaven on Earth.

Figure 149 Windy Point Cumbres - Garcia Collection

This old photo shows the railroad tracks, and you can vaguely see the train making its way up Windy Point. The road following closely was the old Toll Road that Mr. Gus Jenkins had built to accommodate travel between Antonito, CO and Chama, NM. Later the State Highway Department would use this road to build a highway.

Battle of Cumbres

The other interesting fact about this particular area is that the Battle of Cumbres was fought here in July of 1848. The Utes and Apache had been raiding the Taos Pueblo and Major W. W. Reynolds, commander of a company of Union Army soldiers, was ordered to go after them. He took with him Bill Williams, the famous scout from North Carolina because he was very familiar with this part of the country. The river in Arizona along with the town of Williams are named after him.

The campaign against the Apache's and Utes started in Taos. Ultimately, the Ute and Apache made a stand at Cumbres Pass and when it was over thirty-six Native Americans and two Union Soldiers lost their lives in the battle. Many more on both sides were wounded. Bill Williams who was married to a Ute woman and a friend to the Utes got injured and lost favour with them.

Later in the same year while he was at Bent's Fort, he joined a team for Mr. Fremont to try and find a suitable pass for a railroad through the Sangre de Cristo's. Once they got going, he advised Mr. Fremont to turn back because winter was quickly approaching. They didn't take his advice and eleven men lost their lives. The next year he went back to the area near Del Norte to see if they could find survivors. He lost his life to a Ute brave on March 21, 1849. Oddly enough he was buried, and his life celebrated, by the Utes.

Homestead of Cumbres

I've been asked "how did the Garcia's end up with Cumbres?" It was the same question I asked my father. He told me that the Tierra Amarilla Land Grant took in all that was the Chama River watershed which included Wolf Creek. When they started surveying the Land Grant, they came to Cumbres, and instead of going around the basin they cut across and left this beautiful piece of property. Our grandfather, Jose Amarante Garcia used to contract with Mr. Thomas Catron who at one time was the owner of most of the grant to graze his sheep. So, when he found out what had taken place, he homesteaded what we now know as Cumbres.

The railroad made it possible to have a person live on the property for a whole year. He homesteaded his first one hundred and sixty acres by building a cabin and having a man live there. He quickly followed up with a second one-hundred-and-sixty-acre parcel that included the area where the lake and cabin are located. The lake was dredged out using horses and the cabin was built in 1912. The lake is continually fed by a spring that has the purest and coldest water.

Figure 150 Jose Amarante on the left at the cabin - Garcia Collection

Figure 151 Garcia Lake Cumbres - Garccia Collection

Maria Rosa Villapando

MARIA ROSA VILLALPANDO WAS BORN ON OCTOBER 12, 1738 in San Juan, New Mexico. She is our 5th great-grandmother on the Jaquez side of the family. In August of 1760 the Comanche attacked her father's settlement in Ranchos de Taos while he was gone and killed all the men including her husband Juan Jose Jaquez, but her son Jose Julian survived. We have to assume that her father raised the boy when he returned to the hacienda and found him.

Figure 152 Maria Rosa Villapando - New Mexico Historic Women

Along with about sixty other women and children, they took her captive and after about eight years she was sold to the Kiowa. During that time, she had a son with one of the Comanches and named him, Antoine Xavier. After being with the Kiowa for a couple of years, a French trapper and trader by the name of Jean Bapiste de Sale dit LaJoie discovered her while he was trading with the Indians. He ransomed her and together they had another son by the name of Jean Bapiste Lambert. He took Rosa, along with her two sons, to the small village of St. Louis, Missouri where he was based and married her in 1870. I was told they were one of the founding families of the city of St. Louis. She had two more children with Pierre, Helene Joseph and Marie Joesphe.

Figure 153 New Mexico Historical Marker

After twenty-two years of marriage her husband Jean Bapiste moved back to France and never returned to St. Louis. From what I have been able to research, it seems he also left her with a certain amount of wealth. Her family was quite well to do in the city of St. Louis.

Her son Jose Julian discovered his mother was still alive and living in St. Louis, so he set out to find her. She acknowledged that he was her son and gave him two hundred dollars to settle his inheritance. He returned to New Mexico and, sad to say, was somewhat of a derelict abandoning his wife and children for a time. Eventually he got himself together and got back with his wife and children.

One of his children was Felipe De Jesus the first and he was the father of my great- great-grandfather, Jose Maria Jaquez.

Her grandson from her daughter Helene was the famous scout, trapper and landowner, Antoine Leroux. He married Juana Catarina Vigil on November 4, 1833 and became the principal owner of the 426,024-acre Los Lutero's Land Grant which became known as the Antoine Leroux Land Grant.

Maria Rosa would pass away at over a hundred years of age leaving behind a multitude of New Mexico families. She is buried under the St. Louis Arch, at the Basillica of St. Louis. Maria Rosa has a dedication site at both the arch and a highway marker south of Taos.

Vigil Family

THIS SECTION WILL CONTAIN INFORMATION and photos of our mom's side of the family, the Vigils. We didn't have a lot of pictures of my mother's side of the family, but we did manage to get some to identify our aunt and uncles.

Simeon Turley

TO START WITH, THE VIGIL FAMILY is actually part of the Turley family. We will begin with the history of Simeon Turley. The photo below is of a distant cousin of Simeon's, Jonathan Turley, who also owned a mill in southern Indiana at a place called Spring Creek. He lived about the same time as Simeon and I wanted to see what a Turley looked like back then. So please do not confuse the two.

Figure 154 Jonathan Turley
- Garcia Collection

Simeon was born in 1805 at Tate's Creek, Madison County, Kentucky to Benjamin Turley and Nancy Ann Noland. Benjamin served as a private during the American Revolutionary War for Independence under Colonel Archibald Orme's Regiment, Middle Battalion, Montgomery County, Maryland.

Benjamin was born on April 28, 1762 in Frederick County, Maryland to Thomas Turley and Elizabeth Losey. He passed away on April 17, 1812 in Madison County, Kentucky. Simeon's mother Nancy Ann Noland was born on July 14, 1765 in Montgomery, Maryland to Stephen Noland I and Mary Mallot. She passed away on November 1, 1791 in Madison, KY.

We trace the Turley's back to James I born in 1703 in Prince George, Maryland. I believe his father was John Turley and they migrated from England. My mom often mentioned that we were

Irish but after doing some research it seems that the Turleys were more English than Irish.

The Turleys eventually immigrated to Missouri and one account I read mentioned that Jesse, along with his brother Stephen, led a caravan from Missouri in 1826 and brought a young sixteen-year-old Kit Carson to New Mexico. Once the trade route between Missouri and Santa Fe and Taos had been established, the brothers began to ship goods and eventually took their young brother Simeon to Taos. Between 1827 and 1829 Simeon moved to Arroyo Hondo and proceeded to purchase land for farming and raising stock. He built a grist mill and a distillery and produced a whiskey known as "Taos Lightning," and it was flavoured with chili powder, gun powder and tobacco. There was a strict enforcement of U. S. regulations which forbade selling liquor to Indians. Since his property was on New Mexican soil, people from all over sought out Turley's Mill, eventually making him one of the richest men in New Mexico. Oddly enough I remember my mother telling me that he was one of the wealthiest men in New Mexico.

He was good friends with the Bent brothers, St. Vrain and the Autobees and began trading with them by sending goods to Bent's Fort on the Arkansas River near Pueblo. When we visited Bent's Fort in May of 2018, one of the interpreters for the Fort brought out a letter that was addressed to Simeon Turley from the Bent St. Vrain Trading Company that was dated in 1847 warning of an uprising that was taking place in Taos.

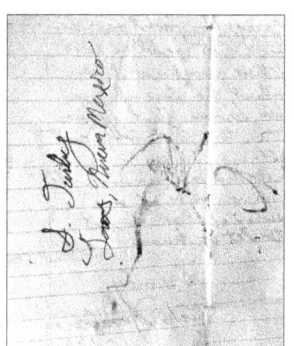

Figure 155 Letter - Garcia Collection

I understand that Simeon was a very generous man and paid his hired help better than most people did at the time. The locals were warm and friendly to him, and he was accepted into the community. He was flourishing in 1846 when the Mexican American War broke out and the United States took possession over the New Mexico territory.

Opposition began to brew, and before long there was a revolt that started on January 19, 1847 in Taos. The mob killed then Governor Charles Bent and several other authorities, and then headed for

Turley's Mill at Arroyo Hondo. They had promised themselves to kill all the Anglos they could find.

Figure 156 Bent's Old Fort National Historic Site

Figure 157 Turley Mill Ruins – Garcia Collection

Charles Autobee, who was returning from Santa Fe on a whiskey delivery, upon hearing about the insurrection raced to Arroyo Hondo to warn Simeon about what was going to happen. Simeon believed that because he had become part of the local fabric they would leave him alone. After discussing with the men who were with him, they decided to close the gates in the outer stockade and pile logs to barricade the entrances to the buildings. It wasn't long before a mob of five hundred Native Americans and Mexicans arrived early on the morning of January 20th.

Simeon was told to surrender the men who were with him and nothing would happen to him. He responded that he would not, and they would have to come and get them. Shots were fired and a battle ensued lasting all day and through the night. By the evening of the second day the mob was able to get into the mill and set fire to it. Most of the men had been killed, and it was decided to dig a hole through one of the walls and escape. Tom Tobin, who later would be known for hunting down the Espinoza brothers, made it to Santa Fe. John Albert was able to escape to the El Pueblo in Colorado, Antoine Le Blanc to the Greenhorn. Simeon managed to get out and was going down the road when a man he knew happened to come along. He offered him his gold watch if he would give him his horse. Instead, the man said he would go and get help. He came back with a mob, and they quickly killed him. Simeon is buried in the Kit Carson Memorial Cemetery in Taos along with the six other men who died at the mill.

Simeon had a sheepherder by the name of Jose Antonio Vigil who was married to a Maria Rosa Romero. Together they had four children: Maria Alveria, Maria Pabla, Jose Andres and Tomacita. Sometime before 1839 Jose Antonio left Maria Rosa and eventually was killed at the Picuris Indian Pueblo in 1845. She and Simeon got together and had three children: Juan De Dios, Jose Manuel and Jose Narcisco. The children never took the name of Turley and kept their mother's married name of Vigil. There are no records to indicate that Rosa was ever married to Simeon.

Juan De Dios was born in April 30,1840 in Arroyo Hondo and his baptismal record indicates that Antonio was his father and since his mother was technically still married to him that makes sense. He married Encarnacion Marquez, and they had they had nine children: Casimira, Juana, Jose Victoriano, Jose Antonio, Jose Ramon, our great, grandfather, Tomas Jose, Juan Antonio, Francisquita and Jose Zacarias. One of those children being Tomas Vigil. Encarnacion passed away about 1882 in Capulin. He then married Bibiana Valdez on March 13, 1884 in Conejos. They had seven children: Placida, Amarante, Maria Sofia Louisa, Elugina, Prestina, Maria Sara and Virginia.

Tomas Jose Vigil

OUR GREAT-GRANDFATHER, TOMAS VIGIL was born on December 22, 1871 in Arroyo Hondo, New Mexico. His father was Juan De Dios, and

Figure 158 Tomas & Anastasia - Garcia Collection

Figure 159 Adelina & Tomas - Garcia Collection

his mother was Encarnacion Marquez. He married Maria Anastasia Sena on October 10, 1892 in Capulin, Colorado. Her father was Jose Tiburcio Sena, who came from a very prominent family that had extensive land holdings in Santa Fe, New Mexico.

They had one child, my grandfather, Guillermo, and Anastasia passed away December of 1919. Tomas met and married Adelina Chavez on June 5, 1920, in Capulin, CO.

Together they had two girls and two boys. The two girls were Del Marie who married Raymond Bustos, and Cecilia and she married Pedro Pollock. The two boys were Ernest who was married to Petra Mondragon and Edward Louis who was married to Stephania Van de Sluis.

Actually, I did not know my grandfather had step-brothers and sisters until I started doing genealogy on the family.

My great-grandfather heard about the Frenchmen who were

Figure 160 Del Marie Bustos - Garcia Collection

Figure 161 Cecilia Pollack -

coming from California with a lot of gold. They were met by the Ute Indians as they were crossing the San Juans and had to bury the gold. Every summer, Tomas would organize a group of men and they headed to the mountains to look for the gold. My grandfather and older uncles would join in, but they never did find it.

Tomas started working on the farm with his father and then eventually bought his own farm in Capulin. He moved to Dragerton, Utah from Capulin to work in the coal mines and was still working at the age of seventy. On May 9, 1945, an explosion took place at the Sunnyside Coal Mine in Carbon County killing 23

Figure 162 Ernest Vigil - Garcia Collection

Figure 163 Edward Vigil - Garcia Collection

miners. Investigators believe the cause was leaking methane gas and unfortunately our great-grandfather Tomas was one of the twenty-three that was killed in that explosion.

Interesting story at the funeral. Uncle Tony was about five years old when his grandfather died in the mine explosion. He remembers his mom trying to get him to kiss his grandfather in the casket. That experience was etched in his memory forever!

Maria Anastasia Sena

MARIA ANTASTASIA WAS BORN APRIL 22, 1877 in Alamosa, Colorado and her parents were Jose Tiburcio Sena and Maria Iginia Gallardo. An interesting note about our Sena family. Our 8th great-grandfather Bernadino Sena was buried under the altar in the San Miguel Chapel in Santa Fe, NM, November 11, 1765. It is the oldest church structure in the United States built circa 1610.

The photo below is Maria Anastasia on the left and her friend, Ortencea Gerard Valdez. Our mom would often mention that her grandmother had a very tiny waist and that she had red hair.

Tiburcio was married to Maria Iginia Gallardo in 1865 in New Mexico. They had eleven children: Valentine, Maria, Maria Clarita, Fermin, Marianne, Maria Anastasia, Benito, David, Guadalupe, Antonio and Solomon. Maria Iginia passed away sometime before 1890 in Colorado. He then married Maria Teresita Archuleta, January 9, 1890 in Antonito. They had seven children: Sofia, Crestina, Euphemia, Maria Felecita, Jose Solomon, Candido and Alberto.

Figure 164 Maria Anastasia Sena - Garcia Collection

Figure 165 Gallardo Family - Garcia Collection

Tiburcio's wife is the girl between her parents. Maria Iginia and her parents are Jose Francisco (Pancho) Gallardo and Encarnacion Valdez. Francisco was born in 1823 in Mexico and Encarnacion was born in1836 in Taos, New Mexico.

Guillermo Vigil

Our grandfather Guillermo on his wedding day.

Figure 166 Guillermo Vigil - Garcia Collection

I was fortunate to get this photo of our grandfather with his father, Tomas and his mother Anastasia.

Figure 167 Guillermo with his father and Mother
- Garcia Collection

Following his father's footsteps, he started farming in Capulin where he met our grandmother Sofia Garcia. They were married June 24, 1916, in Alamosa Colorado. Together they raised a family of eight children. Fernando, Anastasia (our mother,) Valentin, Feliciano,

Figure 168 Guillermo with Kris
- Garcia Collection

Benjamin, Dilia, Amos and Tony. They lost a little girl named Loretta when she was an infant.

They moved to Drageton, Utah where grandfather worked in the coal mines. He retired from the mines and unfortunately passed away at the age of sixty-two. From what my uncles mentioned to me, my grandfather used to laugh and tell jokes. He was very outgoing and loved his wife immensely.

The photo in Figure 169 was taken at his cousin's Felicita Sena and Preciliano Lopez's wedding on November 26, 1926 at Our Lady of Guadalupe church in Conejos, Colorado.

Figure 169 Sena Wedding - Garcia Collection

Sofia Garcia Vigil

SOFIA GARCIA WAS BORN ON NOVEMBER 15, 1895 in Pojoaque, New Mexico. Her father was Ramon Garcia and her mother was Maria Juana Romero.

Figure 170 Sofia on wedding day - Garcia Collection

Our grandmother always wore dresses and carried a handkerchief up her sleeves in the winter.

Figure 171 Sofia with her mother Maria Juana Romero
- Garcia Collection

Sofia's father migrated from Pojoaque, New Mexico to the San Luis Valley and acquired a couple of nice parcels of land in the Capulin and La Jara Canyon area where he would raise livestock and farm.

When Sofia was eleven, her mother passed away. Her father then remarried a lady by the name of Juana Maria Dominguez and together they had two more children: Adela whom it seems died at a very early age and Francisco who was named after his grandfather, Jose Franciso. Juana Maria passed away shortly after Francisco's birth, and Ramon met and married a lady by the name of Rosa Valdez. They never had any children of their own.

Our grandmother was sixty when her husband passed away from the black lung disease that he acquired while working the mines. She passed away on June 18, 1992 in Price, Utah just shy of being ninety-seven. She never married again although she had many suitors. She often mentioned when asked why she wouldn't remarry, she would reply with, "I don't want to wash some old guy's underwear!"

Figure 172 Sofia Vigil - Garcia Collection

*Figure 173 Sofia with her grandchildren, Kris & Michael
- Garcia Collection*

Jose Francisco Garcia

THE BELOW PHOTO IS THE ONLY PHOTO I have been able to acquire of our great-grandfather, Ramon Garcia. I was told that each of his three weddings was a spectacular event.

Figure 174 Great-grandfather Ramon on right - Garcia Collection

The photo shows my brothers Cas and Tom on the truck and my mother holding me, next to her is Rosa and the little girl is Kris. I believe the photo was taken in Capulin, Colorado.

I've been able to trace this line of Garcia's all the way back to Juan Garcia De La Mora who was born in 1670 in Almagro, Ciudad Real, Castilla-La Mancha, Spain.

Every time my grandmother would come to see our family, she would try to make it to Capulin to see her dad and young brother.

Uncle Francisco (Frank) was born on Feb 18, 1912 in Capulin, Colorado to Ramon Garcia and Juana Maria Dominguez. Looks like he was named after his grandfather, Jose Francisco Garcia.

Frank married his sweetheart Adelina Gomez on January 14, 1935 at the Catholic Church in Antonito, Colorado.

Adelina was born on June 12,1912 in Capulin, Colorado to Jesus Maria Gomez and Francesquita Lucero. She was the oldest of ten children. The other nine were Teodorita, Alberto, Sara, Matthew, Eliviria, Elsie, Juan Benito, Ubaldo and Florida.

Together Frank and Adelina had four children. Estrella, Connie, Valentino and Levi.

Francisco passed away on December 6, 1998 in Capulin, Colorado and Adelina passed away on November 26, 1994 in Capulin, Colorado.

Figure 175 Francisco & Adelina - Garcia Collection

Figure 176 Frank & Adelina - Garcia Collection

Fernando Vigil

OUR MOTHER'S OLDEST BROTHER WAS FERNANDO, and he was born on Oct 9, 1916 in Capulin, CO. Our uncle joined the US Army and fought in World War II. He met and married Dulcinea Munoz from Capulin, CO on November 20, 1945 in Denver, CO.

Together they had twelve children: Margaret, Elanor, Mary Jane, William, Danny, Robert, Rebecca, Vivian, Tommy, Adeline, David and Alice. Uncle Fernando passed away on January 2, 1973 in East Carbon, Utah. His wife Tia Dulcinea is still living with her daughter Eleanor Ortiz and at this writing is ninety-eight years old.

Figure 177 Fernando Vigil
- Garcia Collection

Figure 178 Dulcenea Munoz
- Garcia Collection

Valentin Vigil

MOTHER'S YOUNGER BROTHER following her was Valentin, He was born on November 7, 1921 in Capulin, CO. He met and married Rose Mary Martinez. She was born on October 31, 1935 in Gallup, New Mexico.

They had seven children: Loretta, Sandra, Valentin, Jeffery, Gregory, Ernie, and Rosalind. Uncle Valentin enlisted in the US Army on October 20, 1942 in time for World War II. He passed away on May 31, 1986 in East Carbon, UT. Rosa passed away on June 15, 2001 in Rocky Ford, Colorado.

Figure 179 Rose M Martinez
– Sandra Gomez

Figure 180 Valentin Vigil
- Garcia Collection

Feliciano Vigil

FELICIANO WAS BORN ON FEBRUARY 23, 1924 in Capulin, Colorado. I only got to see my uncle once and that is when we went to Roosevelt, Utah. Our uncle never married, and as far as I know did not have any children. He served in the U.S. Army and worked pastoring sheep and in different mines. He passed away on April 16, 1980 in Vernal UT.

Figure 181 Feliciano Vigil – Garcia Collection

Benjamin Vigil

BENJAMIN WAS BORN ON OCTOBER 11, 1926 in Capulin, CO. Tio Ben always reminded me of Hoss Cartwright from the show Bonanza. He was just jovial, happy, kind of man and we always enjoyed his company.

Figure 182 Corina, Sofia & Ben - Garcia Collection

He like his brother Feliciano did not have any children. He was married later in life to Manny Quintana.

Here is a photo of Uncle Ben with his mother, Sofia and Corina Sena. Uncle Ben and Corina were together for a lot of years. They lived in Rocky Ford, Colorado and her children treated him like their father. The photo on the right is Ben with his mother, Sofia and his sister, Viola.

Figure 183 Corina, Sofia & Ben - Garcia Collection

Viola (Delia) Vigil Valdez

VIOLA WAS BORN ON MAY 8, 1929 in Alamosa, Colorado. She married Joe Valdez on March 17, 1945 in Dragerton, Utah. Together they had four children: Jonnie, Dorothy, Esther and Terry.

The following paragraph was taken from her obituary.

> She loved to travel, camp, fish, crochet, eat out, do puzzles, shop, and spend time with family and friends. She was also an amazing cook, and enjoyed making candy for the holidays. She was a great hostess for the family holidays and was always the classy lady in the room. Jewelry and heels were her thing, along with her great sense of humor and infectious smile that made everyone that met her, love her immediately. She never had enemies only friends. Viola wasn't just a homemaker, but a businesswoman also. She managed several apartments over the years, and her tenants loved her. She went through many trials in life and was a great example of determination.

A story Uncle Tony talks about his sister was that when she was a young girl, she wanted to get married so badly, and her parents didn't want her to. So, she told her mom that she would drink a gallon of Clorox if they didn't let her get married. Grandma told her "go ahead but leave me enough to do the wash."

My wife and I enjoyed our visits with Tia Dilia. Once when I took my mom to visit her, we got there late at night and when she came to the door to meet us, she looked at my mother and cried out, "Mama!" My mother resembled grandma, Sofia so much that in my aunt's eyes she looked just like her.

Figure 184 Joe & Delia Wedding Day - Garcia Collection

I was thankful that she got to share some of the family history with me before she passed.

Joe was born on September 18, 1929 in Red River, New Mexico.

Dilia and Joe Valdez were about sixteen years old when they were married in Dragerton, Utah on March 17, 1945.

The photo below has Leroy, Delia, Terry, Joe and Esther.

Joe passed away on September 9, 2012 in Ogden, UT and Delia passed away on April 19, 2018 in Ogden, UT.

Figure 185 Valdez Family - Garcia Collection

162

Amos Agapito Vigil

AMOS VIGIL WAS BORN ON FEBRUARY 6, 1935 in Capulin, CO. He was married to Glenda Byers and they had four boys: Larry, Tony, Michael and Randy. Amos was a miner

and worked in different locations and different types of mines throughout Utah in his lifetime. He enjoys telling a good joke and having good laugh.

Tio Amos at eighty-six years old.

The photo below is Uncle Amos's nephew, Antonio Jr. his son Tony, his son Michael, his nephew Amos, and his grandnephew, Antonio III. Uncle Amos in front.

Figure 186 Amos Vigil - Garcia Collection

Figure 187 Uncle Amos - Garcia Collection

Antonio Vigil

ANTONIO WAS BORN AUGUST 6, 1940 in Capulin, CO. Tony proudly served in the US Army during the Korean Conflict. He was a coal miner and worked at various mines in both Colorado and Utah. He married Myrtle Morris on June 25, 1973 in Las Vegas, Nevada. They had two sons, Amos and Antonio Jr. He passed away on October 20, 2021 in East Carbon, Utah.

Figure 188 Antonio Vigil & Myrtle Morris
– Garcia Collection

Valdez Family

I WANTED MY GRANDCHILDREN TO KNOW MY WIFE'S side of the family and so I included some of the ancestors from Susanne's family.

*Figure 189 Jose Ubaldo Valdez
- JoAnn Triviso*

*Figure 190 Jose Ubaldo Valdez
- JoAnn Triviso*

Her father was Jose Ubaldo Valdez born April 3, 1921 in La Conova, NM to Juan B Valdez and Ramoncita Duran. He married Mary Grace Lopez on December 18, 1943 in Craig, CO. Together they had eleven children: MaryAnn, William, Johnny, JoAnn, Pete, Diane, RoseAnn, Susanne, Judy Ann, Barbara and Patsy

I've been able to trace the Valdez family back to Juan Domingo Valdez who was born in Santa Cruz, NM around 1696 and his wife was Ana Maria Marquez born in Santa Fe in 1703.

Jose Ubaldo was a manager for the Valley Merchants baseball team. His sons Johnny, Billy and Pete played on this team along with a number of kids from the neighborhood.

Figure 191 Jose Ubaldo Valdez - JoAnn Triviso

Joe was working in Craig, Colorado when he met Mary and their first three children were born in Routt County. Two of their children were born in Velarde, NM. Another two were born in Santa Fe, and the rest were born in Albuquerque, NM. I understand that Jose Ubaldo loved to have a garden and would have his children weed it and water it. He also had a pickup that was named Tootie that he would use to take his kids to Velarde.

Figure 192 Mary & Joe - JoAnn Triviso

Lopez Family

MARY GRACE LOPEZ WAS BORN
ON JUNE 23, 1927 in Velarde,
NM to Anicasio Lopez and
Matilda Gonzales where her
father was working with the
sheep ranches.

The Lopez family was
originally from Penasco, New
Mexico.

Mary always had the pot of
coffee going for whoever would
grace the door of her home.
She was a fantastic cook and
loved to do crossword puzzles.
She passed away at the age of
sixty on October 31, 1987 in
Albuquerque, NM.

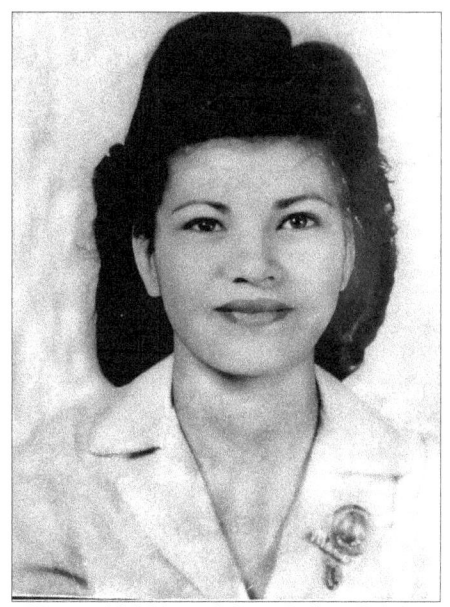

Figure 193 Mary & Joe - JoAnn Triviso

Susanne's grandparents
(Figures 197 & 198) were
Anicasio Lopez and Matilda
Gonzales. Anicasio was born on
December 12, 1892 in Penasco,
NM to Nicanor Lopez and
Maria Barbara Maes. Matilda's
parents were Pedro Gonzales
and Maria Victoria Maesta and
she was born on Feb 8, 1900
also in Penasco, NM.

Anicasio worked on a sheep
ranch in Craig, Colorado and
together with Matilda they had

Figure 194 Mary with Anicasio
- JoAnn Triviso

Figure 195 Valdez Reunion 2018 - Garcia Collection

Figure 196 Valdez Family - Garcia Collection- JoAnn Triviso
– Patsy, Barbara, Judy, Susanne, RoseAnn, JoAnn, Pete, Billy & Johnny.

seven children starting with Virginia, Pemie, Mary Grace, Dora, Amado Roland, Norman and Nick.

Anicasio passed away on March 18, 1954 in Craig, CO and Matilda passed away on April 27, 1979 also in Craig, CO.

Figure 199 is Nicanor Lopez who was born on September 18, 1853 at the Picuris Pueblo in New Mexico. He lived in Penasco and had

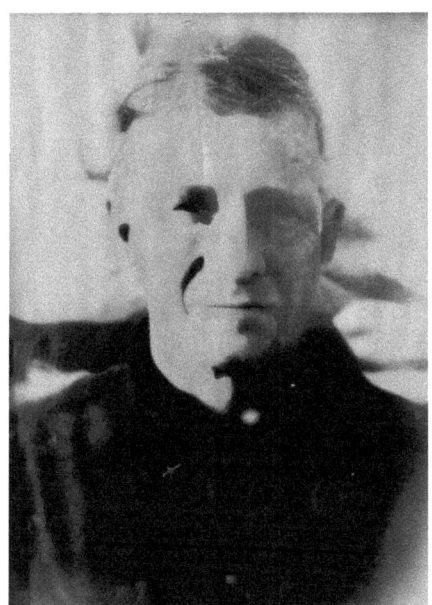

Figure 197 Anicasio Lopez
- JoAnn Triviso

Figure 198 Matilda Gonzales
- Diane Martinez

Figure 199 Nicanor Lopez
– Garcia Collection

extensive land holdings. He was married three times. His first wife was Maria Barbara Maes and they had six children,: Antonio Jesus, Brigido, Demecia, Adelaido, Anicasio, Susanne's grandfather, followed by Emelina. His second wife was Margarita Gonzales and they had one child Jose R. His last wife was Barbara Miera and they had eight children beginning with Juan Jose, Ruperta, Gertrudez, Eloisa, Nicanor, Jubencio, Candido Manuel and Leonicio.

Figure 200 Lopez Family - JoAnn Triviso

On the top row is Dora, Mary, Virginia, Pemie and Roland. Bottom row is Norman, Anicasio, Nick and Matilda.

Figure 201 Valdez Family - Garcia Collection

Above is a photo of the wedding day for Patsy Valdez and Dave Ortiz. Left to right: Barbara, Joni, JoAnn, Pete, Mary Ann, the bride Patsy, the mother Mary, Diane, William, Susanne, Judy and RoseAnne.

Figure 202 Johnny & Jessica - JoAnn Triviso

On the above the photo one brother is missing and that is Johnny. He is with his daughter Jessica.On the above the photo one brother is missing and that is Johnny. He is with his daughter Jessica.

Figure 203 Lopez Family Reunion 2016 - Garcia Collection

Elizabeth Miller Garcia

BETH, AS WE AFFECTIONATELY KNEW OUR SISTER-IN-LAW, came into our lives when she married our brother Cas on April 1, 1967, in Klamath Falls, Oregon. She was born Feb 1, 1944 in Chicago, Illinois. She passed away on Mar 3, 2016 in Manassa, CO. Below is her obituary.

Retired Judge Beth Garcia passes away

CONEJOS COUNTY — Retired Conejos County Judge Mary Elizabeth "Beth" Garcia, 72, passed away on Thursday, March 3.

Governor Ritter appointed Judge Garcia to the Conejos County bench in September 2007 and retained in 2010. She retired in August 2013.

Garcia earned a Bachelor of Arts degree in history and English from Adams State College in Alamosa in 1965 and a law degree from the University of Denver College of Law in Denver in 1980.

Garcia was a partner in private practice with Garcia Law Practice in Alamosa and a part time Municipal Judge for the town of La Jara, Conejos County, Colorado. She handled a civil practice with an emphasis in family law for more than 20 years. She was a member of the Colorado Bar Association.

A resident of Manassa, she had lived in Conejos County since 1983 and was involved in San Luis Valley community organizations such as the Boys and Girls Club. Before going into law, Garcia had worked at the Valley Courier.

She is survived by husband Castelar "Cas" and daughter Victoria, who is also an attorney.

Funeral arrangements are pending with Romero Funeral Home of Alamosa.

Courtesy photo
Mary Elizabeth Garcia

Figure 204 Beth Miller Garcia - Garcia Collection

Tomas Evon Garcia

OUR SECOND OLDEST BROTHER TOM was born on January 7, 1942 in Alamosa, Colorado. He graduated from Antonito High School and went on to attend Adams State College. He eventually earned his Bachelor's Degree and also a Certification for Dismantling Nuclear Facilities. He married Barbara Cole on October 28, 1973 in Shreveport, LA. Tom and Barbara raised two boys: Ricky and Timothy. He brought a lot of joy and laughter into our lives and we miss him a lot. Tom passed away on December 14, 2012 in Clemmons, NC.

Figure 205 Tom & Barbara - Garcia Collection

About the Author

MICHAEL R. GARCIA WAS BORN IN THE SAN LUIS VALLEY and attended Conejos Elementary School until the fourth grade and then transferred to the Antonito schools and graduated from Antonito High School in 1971. He then enlisted in the US Navy where he was trained to work on data processing equipment and operate large scale computers. Following his military service, he attended Adams State College and then moved to Denver and attended Metropolitan State College. He started his technical career with the City and County of Denver as a computer operator. He was accepted into the Computer Programmer Trainee program. After his training and a budget cut, he transferred over to Denver Department of Social Services where he worked as an information systems analyst.

Figure 206 Michael & Susanne - Garcia Collection

In 1983 an opening for a Programmer Analysts became available at Lowry Air Force Base working on the Air Force Pay system. From 1983 until 2012 he worked on the Military Pay System as a software engineer and systems analyst. He moved to Indianapolis in 2009 and retired November 2012 as Manager of Software Engineering for the Defense Joint Military Pay System (DJMS.) Upon retiring Michael and his wife Susanne moved to Pueblo West, CO in 2013.

Susanne worked in the travel industry and enjoyed fulfilling people's dream vacations. They were married on January 1, 1979 in Craig, CO. They have two children, Kristina married to Patrick Morelli and Michael who is married to Angela Maestas. They have five grandchildren, Isabela, Ameya, Olivia, Sierra and Luciana. Together they enjoy spending time with the family, traveling, camping, and going for walks and hikes. Michael enjoys reading, genealogy, history and researching his family. I hope this book will be a blessing to you and that hopefully we can put a face to a name. God Bless!

Figure 207 Our daughter, Kristina, Isabela, Luciana & Patrick
- Garcia Collection

Figure 208 Our son Michael with Angela, Ameya, Sierra & Olivia
- Garcia Collection

Figure 209 The Garcia Family
- Garcia Collection

Bibliography

Antonito Ledger News – 1898 & 1905

Biographies of Hispanics in the Colorado Legislature Defying the Inquisition in Colonial New Mexico (2018) Francisco Lameli

Diary of the Jesuit Residence of Our Lady of Guadalupe Parish Conejos, Colorado (1982) – Stoller, Steele, Fernandez

Empire Magazine (1996)

Forgotten Cucharenos of the Lower Valley (2010) – Virginia Sanchez

Harvard Classics (1909)

Jose Eusequio Jaquez (2015) – Nora Jacquez

Pleas and Petitions (2021) – Virginia Sanchez

Southern Colorado Register 1946)

The Denver Public Library, *Western History Collection*

The Folklore of Spain in the American Southwest (1985) – Aurelio Espinosa/Jose Manuel Espinosa

The Life and Times of Commander E. C. Cortez (1996) – David Wilde

www.ingramcontent.com/pod-product-compliance
Lightning Source LLC
Chambersburg PA
CBHW051520120626
46551CB00012B/1005